Professionalism in Psychiatry

Professionalism in Psychiatry

by

Glen O. Gabbard, M.D.
Laura Weiss Roberts, M.D., M.A.
Holly Crisp-Han, M.D.
Valdesha Ball, M.D.
Gabrielle Hobday, M.D.
Funmilayo Rachal, M.D.

American
Psychiatric
Publishing
A Division of American Psychiatric Association

Washington, DC
London, England

Copyright © 2012 American Psychiatric Association
ALL RIGHTS RESERVED

Manufactured in the United States of America on acid-free paper
15   14   13   12   11   5   4   3   2   1
First Edition

Typeset in Bembo.

American Psychiatric Publishing,
a Division of American Psychiatric Association
1000 Wilson Boulevard
Arlington, VA 22209-3901
www.appi.org

Library of Congress Cataloging-in-Publication Data
Professionalism in psychiatry / by Glen O. Gabbard ... [et al.]. — 1st ed.
    p. ; cm.
    Includes bibliographical references and index.
    ISBN 978-1-58562-337-2 (pbk. : alk. paper) 1. Psychiatry—Practice.
2. Professional ethics. 3. Physician and patient. I. Gabbard, Glen O.
    [DNLM: 1. Psychiatry—standards. 2. Ethics, Professional. 3. Professional
Competence—standards. 4. Professional Practice—standards. 5. Professional-
Patient Relations. WM 21]
    RC440.8.P77 2012
    616.890068—dc23

                                                                2011026350

British Library Cataloguing in Publication Data
A CIP record is available from the British Library.

Contents

About the Authors

Valdesha Ball, M.D., is Clinical Assistant Professor of Psychiatry at Baylor College of Medicine in Houston, Texas.

Holly Crisp-Han, M.D., is Clinical Assistant Professor of Psychiatry at Baylor College of Medicine in Houston, Texas; and Candidate at the Center for Psychoanalytic Studies in Houston, Texas.

Glen O. Gabbard, M.D., is Professor of Psychiatry at SUNY Upstate Medical University in Syracuse, New York; Clinical Professor of Psychiatry at Baylor College of Medicine in Houston, Texas; and Training and Supervising Analyst at the Center for Psychoanalytic Studies in Houston, Texas.

Gabrielle Hobday, M.D., is Clinical Assistant Professor of Psychiatry at Baylor College of Medicine in Houston, Texas.

Funmilayo Rachal, M.D., is Forensic Psychiatry Fellow in the Department of Psychiatry and Behavioral Sciences at Emory University School of Medicine in Atlanta, Georgia.

Laura Weiss Roberts, M.D., M.A., is Chairman and Katharine Dexter McCormick and Stanley McCormick Memorial Professor in the Department of Psychiatry and Behavioral Sciences at Stanford University School of Medicine in Stanford, California.

Disclosures of Competing Interests

The following contributor disclosed forms of support that could present or appear to present competing interests with regard to work published in this volume, as follows:

Laura Weiss Roberts, M.D., M.A.–The author owns a small business, Terra Nova Learning Systems, that builds science-based education products. She receives competitive federal grants. She does not personally receive drug company or industry dollars.

The following contributors reported that they had no competing interests to declare:

Valdesha Ball, M.D.
Holly Crisp-Han, M.D.
Glen O. Gabbard, M.D.
Gabrielle Hobday, M.D.
Funmilayo Rachal, M.D.

Introduction

In American society, the physician has always been regarded as a professional. Psychiatrists, by virtue of being specialists in medicine, also regard themselves as professionals. Nonetheless, in the past, professional behavior was rarely defined and variably practiced. Physicians who exploded at nurses were tolerated and seldom disciplined. Some physicians and psychiatrists responded to phone calls and pages, and others did not. Few doctors of any specialty endorsed quality improvement efforts, and many resented hospital administrators who attempted to implement such measures in the facility where the doctors worked. A great deal of unprofessional behavior was tolerated that involved insensitive interactions with patients, families, and coworkers. The perceived power of physicians had an intimidating effect on those with whom they worked. Many would be afraid to confront insensitive and boorish behaviors because of the potential for repercussions. Instead, the unprofessional instances of outbursts and irresponsibility were contextualized with comments such as, "Well, that's just the way Dr. Smith is. We can't expect him to change." Physicians themselves might comment on their own behaviors with similar resignation: "That's the way I was trained. Everyone treated me badly, so now I'm treating others the way I was treated. It's a rite of passage."

Times have changed. The rise of professionalism within medicine in general and psychiatry in particular has swept through organized medicine in a way that has prompted a quiet revolution in how doctors are trained and how they are expected to behave in the workplace. The Accreditation Council for Graduate Medical Education (ACGME) has advanced professionalism to one of the six domains of competence, or "core competencies." Now a physician's skill in the operating room or in diagnosis must be accompanied by a range of professional behaviors that include such things as being a good team player, being accountable, pursuing improvement in an ongoing way, behaving compassionately toward patients and families, treating all coworkers with respect, and even being attuned to the management of healthcare resources in a manner that reflects fairness and integrity.

Physicians must report colleagues who are impaired or incompetent. They must commit to treating patients from all ethnic groups, races, and sexual orientations with the same high level of integrity and ethics. Confidentiality must be rigorously preserved. Physicians must make themselves accessible to patients. These professional behaviors are measured and quantified, and corrective actions may be taken when they are breached.

Although almost all physicians believe in professionalism, the movement toward making professionalism a core competency has challenged doctors everywhere to accept the practice of monitoring, observing, and assessing that is not always welcome in a field in which autonomy is highly valued.

Psychiatry presents a special challenge in defining and implementing professionalism because of the unusual focus on the doctor-patient relationship and the privacy required for psychiatric treatment to be effective. So much depends on the character of the psychiatric resident or graduate psychiatrist. Moreover, negative feelings toward patients are not simply suppressed or disavowed but rather are viewed as important information that must be taken into account in understanding the patient's personality and the psychiatrist's contribution to the two-person field.

Because the challenges of applying principles of professionalism to psychiatry are formidable, we have attempted a systematic examination of professional values and behaviors as they apply to psychiatry. Diversity in gender, culture, age, race, religion, and sexual orientation requires psychiatrists to be especially sensitive and empathic. Hence we have assembled a group of co-authors that feature diversity in a way that is perhaps unusual for psychiatric textbooks. In the ensuing chapters, multiple voices are blended to articulate the new professionalism that psychiatry is embracing while recognizing that it is not a matter of "one size fits all" thinking. Professionalism must be approached with flexibility and with the knowledge that it is evolving in ways that may be unforeseen. The rise of the Internet has radically changed society and has placed new demands on psychiatrists to think about professionalism in cyberspace. The acceptance of multiculturalism as the fundamental character of American society has also required responses within psychiatry. The enormous influence of gender studies and the increasing gender balance in the psychiatric workforce have produced changes in the practice of psychiatry that must be addressed as matters of professionalism.

All of these dimensions that have shaped the face of American psychiatry are taken up in this volume with the intent of forging a beginning effort to place these many issues in a systematic framework. Our views of professionalism in psychiatry are not definitive but are our best efforts at this time to characterize the professional behaviors and clinical strategies of the contemporary psychiatrist. We know that the views expressed here will continue to evolve.

We would like to thank a number of individuals who have helped with this project. Robert Hales and John McDuffie were patient and supportive as we took our time trying to map uncharted waters. Diane Trees-Clay and Ann Tennier ably assisted the authors in collecting references, organizing large amounts of data, and typing manuscripts. Greg Kuny and his coworkers at American Psychiatric Publishing took the raw manuscript and transformed it into the final publication that you now hold in your hands. Our heartfelt gratitude goes out to all these individuals who made this project possible.

Glen O. Gabbard, M.D.
Laura Weiss Roberts, M.D., M.A.
Holly Crisp-Han, M.D.
Valdesha Ball, M.D.
Gabrielle Hobday, M.D.
Funmilayo Rachal, M.D.

Chapter 1

Professionalism in Medicine and Psychiatry

Scenario 1

Dr. Alberts, a 47-year-old psychiatrist, was called in from home to see a long-standing patient who had just been admitted to an acute psychiatric inpatient unit. According to the family, the patient had "once again refused to take his medication." This was a familiar story for Dr. Alberts, who was "completely exasperated." He had struggled for a number of years to establish a therapeutic alliance with this patient in the hope that he would see the value of taking medication and adhering to the treatment plan.

Dr. Alberts burst onto the unit, strode up to the charge nurse, and asked curtly, "Where's Gene?" The nurse looked worried and responded, "Mr. McDonald is in Room 612, but I wouldn't see him right now if I were you. He's actively hallucinating—he seems really scared, really frightened." Dr. Alberts, with evident frustration, retorted, "I didn't ask you your opinion! I just asked what room he was in."

He then walked down the hall to Room 612 and opened the door without knocking. The patient was curled up in a ball on his bed in the corner of the room and said, "I'm sorry Dr. Alberts. The pills you made me take were poisoning my system...my bowels have traces of alien substances I've never seen before." Still standing in the doorway, the psychiatrist frowned and demanded, "How many times do I have to tell you,

Gene? The pills aren't poison. They're what keeps you out of a hospital—and yet you refuse to take them! I honestly don't know what I'm
going to do with you!" He took a few steps into the room.

The patient looked more frightened and said, "The pills *are* poison-
ous! That's why my bowels don't work properly!"

Dr. Alberts' voice became shrill: "You think that because you have
schizophrenia!"

"I do *not* have schizophrenia! I know what I'm talking about!" the
patient responded.

"Well, what else do you call somebody who thinks voices are talking
to him when no one's there and gets paranoid about poison in his bowel
movements?" the psychiatrist asked sarcastically. He then turned and
went to the door. He looked back at the patient, muttering, "I don't believe this." With that, he closed the door and stomped off of the unit.

Scenario 2

After the departure of Dr. Alberts, the charge nurse went into the chart
room and spoke with Dr. Gray, a postgraduate year IV resident doing a
clinical assignment on the inpatient unit. The nurse's voice quavered as
she spoke to Dr. Gray: "I don't want to badmouth Dr. Alberts, but he
really upset Mr. McDonald in Room 612. Would you be willing to have
a chat with Mr. McDonald?"

Dr. Gray looked up from the chart she was reading and replied,
"Sure. I'll be glad to see him."

When she got to Mr. McDonald's room, he was shaking. He looked
up at Dr. Gray and said, "Don't let Alberts near me!"

Dr. Gray replied, "What happened, Mr. McDonald?" She then sat
down to listen.

The patient explained, "He terrorized me. He called me schizo-
phrenic and said I was hearing voices."

"Oh, I see," Dr. Gray responded. "That must have hurt your feelings."

"Well, it's not true," Mr. McDonald retorted. "I'm not crazy. I have
alien substances in my stool. I can't help it."

Dr. Gray reflected for a moment. "That must be terrifying. Tell me
all about it."

Over a period of 30 minutes, Mr. McDonald told Dr. Gray all the
details as she listened empathically. He calmed down eventually, and
Dr. Gray got up to leave.

The patient asked, "Where are you going?"

Dr. Gray replied, "Just like you, I need to get some rest. We'll talk
some more in the morning."

Two situations. Both commonplace. One rich with compassion, kind-
ness, and clinical acumen; the other impoverished of all three. The first the

antithesis of professionalism; the second an exemplar of professionalism.

The first scenario gives a rather appalling account of a clinical interaction—one that is likely to make the reader wince. It is certainly an example of poor treatment. The psychiatrist appears to be unable to handle the adherence problems and frequent relapses common in schizophrenia. His behavior is an intense display of countertransference adversely affecting the patient's care. Moreover, Dr. Alberts' behavior is a clear breach of professionalism. He raises his voice at the patient. He is punitive rather than therapeutic. He blames the patient for his symptoms. He is insensitive in the way he explains the diagnosis to the patient. Furthermore, he is contemptuous and dismissive to one of his coworkers, a nurse on the inpatient unit. A poor role model, Dr. Alberts certainly does not comport himself as a compassionate, respectful expert entrusted with the care of a distressed and seriously ill patient.

In the second example, Dr. Gray is empathic. She is generous with her time and shows a capacity to accept—or perhaps simply to help bear—the patient's suffering. She is able to sit with the hurt and then offer hope, seeking ultimately to serve the well-being and interests of the patient, a young man facing a serious disease. She is respectful and helpful both to the patient and to the nurse. She puts the patient's needs before her own.

We all tend to know professionalism when we see it. We also can spot breaches of professionalism. Faced with developing a succinct definition, however, we may find ourselves stuck. Even if we turn to authoritative sources for definitions, like the *Oxford English Dictionary,* we still may feel that the definition we seek is elusive. A recent edition of that august volume offers the following definition: "The body of qualities or features, as competence, skill, etc., characteristic of a professional" (Brown 1993, p. 2368). We certainly agree with the notions of skill and competence (as explored in Chapter 2), but we find ourselves disappointed with the "etc." Some difficult-to-define qualities intrinsic to professionalism must be included for a well-rounded definition.

Defining the essence of professionalism has become a hot topic in all of medicine in recent years. Professionalism has been elevated to the status of one of the six core competencies in residency training for psychiatrists, and the definition within psychiatry may actually be more complicated than in the rest of medicine. In this chapter we explore the meaning of professionalism first more broadly in medicine and then more narrowly in psychiatry.

Developing a Modern View of Professionalism in Medicine

A doctor does not go through many years of training simply to acquire information and skill—that is the preparation of a technician, not a physician. Indeed, many medical schools have something akin to a "white coat ceremony" early in training. This ceremony is not an empty ritual but a way of connoting that becoming a doctor entails the development of a new identity. It is acknowledged that a set of qualities, professional duties, and behaviors specific to the profession constitutes the essence of that identity—but what exactly are those qualities, duties, and behaviors?

Codes of ethics based on historical perspectives on professionalism emphasize the two positive commitments of a profession: first, to provide unique expertise for the benefit of others in society, and second, to ensure that all members of the profession perform their responsibilities with sufficient knowledge and skill and with the motivation to bring good in serving the interests of others. In other words, there is the responsibility to do good and to ensure that colleagues do as well. However, the search for a current consensus on the meaning of professionalism in the everyday activities of a "professional" has been challenging. For instance, ethical conduct as articulated in the Hippocratic writings included beneficence ("I come for the benefit of the sick"), avoidance of harm, confidentiality ("What I see in the lives of men, I will not noise abroad"), and performance of work only in areas of competence. It also included proscriptions against exploitation of patients ("mischief"), euthanasia ("I will not give a deadly drug, nor suggest such a thing"), pregnancy termination ("I will not give a woman an abortive remedy"), and affiliation with those who do not adhere to the Hippocratic way of practice. The manner, or "decorum," of physicians was also defined in the Hippocratic writings as conferring hope and optimism and avoiding a "gloomy" and discouraging manner in interacting with patients. Although some of these approaches would be wholeheartedly embraced in present-day views of the "ideal" for professionalism, others would not.

As a way of addressing the enhanced awareness of professionalism as a core competency in medicine and fostering dialogue on a modern view of what constitutes professionalism, the American Board of Internal Medicine Foundation et al. (2002) established a number of professional responsibili-

TABLE 1–1.   **Professional responsibilities inherent in professionalism (based on American Board of Internal Medicine Foundation et al. charter statement)**

Confidentiality

An effort to improve the quality of care

A commitment to improving access to care

An equitable distribution of limited resources

A commitment to scientific knowledge

Professional competence

Honesty with patients

Appropriate professional boundaries in the doctor-patient relationship

Establishment and maintenance of trust by managing conflicts
    of interest

Source.   American Board of Internal Medicine Foundation et al. 2002.

ties as crucial to the definition (see Table 1–1). This charter statement led to active discussion about the need for the concept of professionalism to be clarified, expanded, and more deeply grounded in the traditions of medicine. Critics (Riser and Banner 2002; Wagner et al. 2007) noted that the role of the physician as a healer was conspicuous in its absence. Indeed, most practicing physicians think of the healing aspects of medicine as fundamental to their identity. Furthermore, the overall conceptualization of the document appeared to deemphasize the role of physician as entrusted with the care of patients and to overemphasize stewardship of scarce healthcare resources, relegating the physician to a role as a resource "manager."

    Another concern raised by readers of the charter was the lack of input from patients, especially in an era of increased consumerism in healthcare delivery (Riser and Banner 2002; Wofford et al. 2004). In one survey of patients regarding their perspectives on healthcare (Wofford et al. 2004), the way that patients were treated by doctors was of greatest concern. Patients complained of being treated with disrespect and contempt, and they also were concerned about poor communication between doctor and patient. Hence, if one focuses on the inverse of these complaints, one could conclude that treating patients with trust and respect, and making an effort to communicate clearly, are essential features of professionalism from a patient's perspective.

Beyond concerns about the evolving perspectives of professional conduct across human history and context, the literature on professionalism in
medicine has also made it clear that physicians at different stages in their
career trajectory regard professionalism differently. Wagner et al. (2007)
conducted eight focus groups to study these differences more systematically. Faculty and residents from the specialties of pediatrics and family
medicine were recruited, as well as medical students in their junior year
clerkship in family medicine. Fifty-one subjects took part in the focus
groups, including 11 faculty members from family medicine and pediatrics,
13 residents from those two specialties, and 16 medical students. Eleven family medicine patients also took part in two different patient groups. Group
leaders held extensive discussions about the nature of professionalism.
When the investigators analyzed the results, they found that certain themes
were common to all groups—namely, focus group participants valued the
doctor-patient relationship, knowledge and technical skills, and character
virtues. Secondary themes common to all groups included the behavior
and importance of peer relationships, the congruence between outward
appearance and personal characteristics, and the uniqueness of medicine as
a profession. Beyond these common themes, however, they found that the
stage of learning had a great deal to do with what was emphasized. Faculty
members stressed the need for maturity. Residents emphasized the professionalism inherent in assuming responsibility for others by being available
constantly. Students were concerned about the possibility of hurting someone and the edict of doing no harm in the practice of medicine. Finally,
patients above all wished to be heard. The relationship aspect of professionalism was emphasized primarily by both patients and students. Residents
seemed to regard knowledge and skill as more important. The investigators
concluded that it is prudent to include the level of training of the professional and the patients' perspective as part of the overall effort to improve
professionalism.

Other studies have found similar developmental patterns in which the
issues that appear most important evolve over the course of training, and
these concerns may change further once physicians have entered clinical
practice in different areas of medicine, including diverse specialties (e.g.,
primary care, psychiatry, surgery), or undertaken work in distinct roles
(e.g., administrative, consultative, scientific, teaching) or in unique settings
(e.g., rural, military). In a study of 610 trainees and faculty at the major academic health sciences center in West Virginia, Nath et al. (2006) found that

differences in identifying behavior as "unprofessional" existed according to educational level (but not age) for behaviors associated with professional responsibility (e.g., a physician with a family obligation wanting to leave an unstable patient in the care of a colleague) and poor self-care (e.g., a pharmacy student who severely overeats, does not exercise, and does not take prescribed blood pressure medication). In a recent survey study of medical students and residents (Roberts et al. 2005a), similarly, it was documented that certain issues, such as reporting and handling of medical mistakes and balancing personal and professional needs, are identified as universally important and as topics for additional learning, whereas others, such as those related to training itself (e.g., learning "on" patients, how one is introduced to patients, mistreatment of trainees) and interactions with others (e.g., dealing with impaired colleagues, speaking with families), become less of a concern over time. Primary care and psychiatric residents express greater interest in learning about topics such as professionalism in caring for the indigent and other vulnerable populations in relation to stigma and in the care of the terminally ill than do residents from other specialties (e.g., anesthesiology, emergency medicine, obstetrics/gynecology, pathology, radiology, surgery) (Roberts et al. 2005b).

Women also appear to view professionalism and ethics differently from their male colleagues. In multiple studies over the past three decades, women assign greater importance to these aspects of clinical medicine, wish to learn more in their training about these topics, indicate that they are more attentive to these considerations in patient care, and yet often feel less skilled in these areas. In one study that involved more than 300 medical students and residents, women expressed greater interest in learning about topics ranging from social responsibilities of the medical profession to everyday practices and behaviors such as giving advice to family members and accepting gifts from patients (Roberts et al. 2005a). In a study of 97 practicing psychiatrists in two states, similarly, women expressed greater concern for being prepared for dealing with clinical mistakes, allocation of scarce resources, informed consent, withholding sensitive information from families and patients, falsifying documents to protect patient confidentiality, interacting with surrogate decision makers, and other topics. Throughout the literature, men also have expressed greater skepticism and less enthusiastic endorsement of the need to address professionalism issues and ethical considerations in clinical medicine and human studies.

Skepticism and Threats to Professionalism

As noted, a focus on professionalism in medicine is clearly not without its critics (see Table 1–2). Sox (2007) compared professionalism to the tradition of guilds originating in medieval Europe. He argued that, like the guilds, medicine is in an intimate relationship with business and government. He perceived a decline in the reputation of the medical profession because of the rising cost of healthcare. This phenomenon has become a paramount concern of both business and government. Sox accused many physicians of disregarding one aspect of the American Board of Internal Medicine charter (referred to earlier). In that charter, physicians are said to have an obligation to think about keeping costs down for everyone concerned when considering whether to order a consultation or a test for a patient in one's office. The charter also recognizes the need to avoid providing unnecessary services as part of a commitment to a reasonable distribution of finite resources. Sox persuasively argued that the medical profession should take a lesson from the guilds lest they follow the fate of the guilds. They either adapt to the needs of the society or wither. Although we do not agree with all that Sox stated, it is true that professions are empowered by society and are entrusted with key duties by society. Failing to align with the needs and expectations of society will lead to erosion and faltering of the profession.

TABLE 1–2. Critiques of principles of professionalism

Lack of patient input into principles

Insufficient attention to "character"

Tendency to overlook subgroups of professionals

Tendency to understate the complexity of professional behavior

Failure to recognize balancing of work and personal life

Failure to take into account economic realities

Lack of emphasis on the need to keep costs down for everyone

Parallels with guilds of the medieval period

Precepts that are widely endorsed but ignored in practice

Another criticism of professionalism is that its precepts are widely accepted in principle but ignored in practice. In a disconcerting survey of internists, cardiologists, family practitioners, pediatricians, surgeons, and anesthesiologists, of whom 1,662 responded, 93% of the physicians supported the notion that errors should be reported (Campbell et al. 2007). Similarly, 96% agreed that when physicians are incompetent or impaired, their colleagues should report them to the licensing board or hospital authorities. However, when it came to implementing these principles, the respondents told a different story. Forty-six percent of them said they had firsthand knowledge of medical errors but chose not to report them. When colleagues were known to be incompetent or impaired, 45% of participants responded that they had declined to report them. Moreover, 36% said they would possibly order a magnetic resonance image for back pain, even if it were not needed, if the patient demanded it.

Some of the respondents advocated behavior that is consensually viewed as unethical. For example, 1 out of 10 doctors admitted violating patient confidentiality. Even more surprising, 9% of the physicians who responded said they thought it was sometimes appropriate to have a sexual relationship with a patient, a practice that is unequivocally unethical in the American Medical Association's ethics code (Myers and Gabbard 2008). These sobering figures underscore a fundamental problem—physicians may say one thing and do another. Hence, some experts have stressed that what really counts in professionalism is how one behaves when no one is looking.

One of the great ironies is that at the very moment that medical educators have chosen to emphasize professionalism as a core competency, the commercialized nature of healthcare is posing major threats to medical professionalism. Arnold Relman (2007), former editor of the *New England Journal of Medicine,* identified the forces that threaten physician professionalism in our current era. In his view, the ideology that privileges helping the patient over economic rewards is an essential component of professionalism but also the part at greatest risk. Emphasizing the work of Freidson (2001), Relman noted that the "soul" of the medical profession is the ethical foundation of medicine—namely, the commitment of physicians to put the needs of patients ahead of personal gain. This fundamental tenet is being eroded because of the commercialism of healthcare, which has a unique role in the United States, unlike any other country in the world. Too many physicians, in Relman's view, have accepted the notion that medical practice is essentially a business that must use the principles of business to make it viable. This conceptual model will erode the moral commitment to patients and professional altruism that are hallmarks of being a physician.

The influence of the pharmaceutical industry has been another factor leading to deprofessionalization, according to Relman. Continuing medical education is heavily influenced by pharmaceutical companies to the point where much of new knowledge is transmitted by corporations that have a vested interest in selling a product. This thorny state of affairs is discussed at greater length in Chapter 7.

Relman insisted that physicians do not have to accept the commercialization and industrialization of healthcare. In his view, medical care must be reconceptualized as an obligation of the society to its members. Everyone deserves, he argued, to have optimal treatment regardless of his or her ability to pay or his or her condition. Political activism is necessary to accomplish such changes, but Relman persuasively argued that medical professionalism is unlikely to survive if the current commercialized healthcare market continues to dominate healthcare delivery.

Professionalism in Psychiatry

When we shift the lens from all of medicine to the unique and relatively small specialty of psychiatry, complexities become even greater. Our starting point is to examine how psychiatric educators have approached the mandate of teaching professionalism. In 1999, the American Council of Graduate Medical Education (www.acgme.org) stressed that there are six areas in which all residents must achieve competence by the time they finish their residency:

1. Patient care that is compassionate, appropriate, and effective for the treatment of health problems and the promotion of health;
2. Medical knowledge about established and evolving biomedical, clinical, and cognate sciences as well as the application of this knowledge to patient care;
3. Practice-based learning and improvement that involves the investigation and evaluation of care for their patients, the appraisal and assimilation of scientific evidence, and improvements in patient care;

TABLE 1–3.   **Attitudes, skills, and knowledge inherent in professionalism (Residency Review Committee)**

A) Respect, compassion, integrity, and honesty

Being responsive to the needs of patients and society that supersede self-interest

Being accountable to patients, society, and the profession

B) High standards of ethical behavior that include respect for patient privacy and/or autonomy

Maintaining appropriate professional boundaries

Understanding the nuances specific to psychiatric practice

C) Sensitivity and responsiveness to a diverse patient population

---

Source.   Adapted from Andrews and Burruss 2004.

4. Interpersonal and communications skills that result in the effective ex-change of information and collaboration with patients, their families, and other health professionals;
5. Professionalism, as manifested through a commitment to carrying out professional responsibilities, adherence to ethical principles, and sensitivity to patients of diverse backgrounds; and
6. Systems-based practice, as manifested by actions that demonstrate an awareness of and responsiveness to the larger context and system of healthcare as well as the ability to call effectively on other resources in the system to provide optimal healthcare.

The Residency Review Committee that is responsible for promulgating these principles among psychiatric educators has gone on to enumerate the particular attitudes, skills, and knowledge inherent in professionalism (see Table 1–3).

The intent is to provide psychiatric training directors and faculty with benchmarks to determine whether competence has been attained in professionalism. These benchmarks, as outlined by Andrews and Burruss (2004), include

1. Respect, compassion, integrity, and honesty; a responsiveness to the needs of patients and society that supersede self-interest; and account-ability to patients, society, and the profession.

2. High standards of ethical behavior, which include respect for patient privacy and/or autonomy; maintaining appropriate professional boundaries; and understanding the nuances specific to psychiatric practice. Programs are expected to distribute to residents and operate in accordance with the American Medical Association's "Principles of Medical Ethics" with "Annotations Especially Applicable to Psychiatry" as developed by the American Psychiatric Association (2001) to ensure that the application and teaching of these principles are an integral part of the educational process.

3. Sensitivity and responsiveness to a diverse patient population including, but not limited to, diversity in gender, age, culture, race, religion, disability, and sexual orientation.

Cultural sensitivity is at the heart of the psychiatrist's professional identity. Psychiatrists attempt to understand patients in their biopsychosocial context, honoring the many factors that shape an individual's life. One cannot completely transcend the influence of one's culture. Psychiatrists, by the very nature of their practice, are prone to think about the uniqueness of each individual and, unlike other physicians, tend to value the multiplicity and complexity of each individual. Patients are not regarded reductionistically and simplistically as a disease process. A psychiatric disorder occurs in a person (Gabbard 2005), a whole and unique person in a rich and multifaceted context. We say more about cultural influences in Chapter 6.

In spelling out the qualities that need to be measured in assessing competency, the Residency Review Committee provides useful guidelines. However, we cannot help but contemplate certain challenges inherent in the psychiatric perspective. Can the qualities embedded in character, such as honesty, integrity, compassion, and respect, be taught if the psychiatric resident does not have these qualities at the beginning of training? Are these qualities a matter of "you either have them or you don't?" Teaching the knowledge and skills aspect of professionalism is far easier than making changes in fundamental character traits.

The mandate that one needs to be responsive to the needs of patients and society in a way that supersedes self-interest is unimpeachable. Yet this goal may be an ideal rather than a reality. Can we ever manage self-interest in a way that is entirely under our control? Isn't self-interest inherent in our roles as healers? Psychiatrists understand that there are unconscious motivations that lead individuals to seek out specific careers. For example, there is self-interest in the wish to make patients better. We feel good about ourselves if our patients do well. There is another form of self-interest inherent in seeing patients—we get paid for it. Hence we cannot eradicate self-interest; we simply try to manage it as best we can.

The study of professional boundary violations (Gabbard 1996) teaches us a lesson we cannot ignore—namely, we are all masters of self-deception. We can rationalize all kinds of behaviors in the best interest of the patient when a careful evaluation by a colleague will see that we are indulging our own wishes. One psychiatrist said that he was having a female patient sit on his lap because she had not received sufficient mothering. He argued that he was being therapeutic by providing a maternal experience for his patient. The patient herself viewed it as a sexual overture and became frightened. In Chapter 3, our discussion of professional boundaries elaborates on this point in greater detail.

The unprofessional behavior of Dr. Alberts described at the beginning of this chapter illustrates the role of countertransference in psychiatric practice. The physician's emotional reaction to the patient is largely neglected in other specialties. A surgeon who is attempting to treat a patient may become angry at the patient's lack of cooperation but would see feelings generated by the interaction as simply an interference that needs to be suppressed. By contrast, psychiatrists consider countertransference to be a useful tool to understand the patient and the doctor-patient relationship. Patients tend to re-create their internal world in the interaction with clinicians, and psychiatrists do the same (Gabbard 1995, 2005). In the optimal situation, Dr. Alberts would have reflected on what he was feeling before enacting it with his patient and with the unit nurse. He might have recognized that his professional self-esteem (i.e., his self-interest) was wounded by the failure of his patient to follow the treatment plan prescribed for him. He reacted with anger because he experienced the lack of adherence as a personal affront.

In discussions of professionalism, whether around gender, cultural sensitivity, sexual orientation, age, or ethnicity, psychiatrists know that everyone has a variety of personal and idiosyncratic reactions to differences in others. We study those reactions to learn more about ourselves and to understand the doctor-patient interaction with greater sophistication. Political "correctness" has no place in the internal world of the psychiatrist. We must allow ourselves to feel whatever we feel and acknowledge whatever we think. Honesty and accurate self-observation are imperative. We certainly do not advocate carrying those thoughts and feelings into actions that are unprofessional and destructive, but we must try to learn from internal signals and not wish them away because they reflect the dark corners of our psyche. Moreover, when we occasionally enact something with the patient that makes us feel guilty, we must try to contextualize that enactment as something specific about the clinical interaction and learn from it.

The Residency Review Committee criteria (see Table 1–3) refer to "understanding the nuances specific to psychiatric practice." Another difference between psychiatry and other medical specialties is that psychiatrists are held to a higher standard. An understanding of the two-person nature of medical practice is viewed as essential in psychiatry. Hence self-reflection is not only recommended as a laudable aspect of professionalism—it is *expected* as part of the psychiatrist's clinical expertise. Psychiatrists must attempt to see how their own subjectivity (e.g., biases, beliefs, culture, politics) may influence the conclusions they reach about their patients. Few other specialties expect such a fine-grained analysis of how the observer affects the observed.

Psychiatry is held to a higher standard in another sense as well. Psychiatrists are far more attuned to the impact of the power differential between doctor and patient than most of the other specialties. They know that the patient's attitudes toward the physician are heavily influenced by early experiences with parents and other authority figures. Qualities may be attributed to the physician that belong to earlier relationships. Transferences may be exploited, as can power imbalance. Psychiatrists see the therapeutic relationship as a basic tool of healing; hence they are perhaps more cautious than other specialists about the potential for taking advantage of the patient. In most academic centers, fundraising from patients is viewed differently in psychiatry than it is in surgery or other procedure-based specialties. Psychiatrists know that accepting gifts can lead to expectations of special treatment. Offering donations can be based on an idealization of the doctor that is unrealistic. Treating patients who are potential donors can cloud the clinician's judgment as well.

Similarly, confidentiality is seen as far stricter in psychiatry than in other specialties. Many patients do not want anyone else to know that they see a psychiatrist, whereas they may boast about the specialist they see for a surgical procedure or for primary care. Although this difference in part reflects the stigma associated with psychiatric care, psychiatrists must nevertheless respect patients' wish for privacy—even to the point of not acknowledging whom they treat.

Professionalism is of utmost importance in psychiatry, a field of medicine that offers unique expertise and serves the well-being of people from all walks of life in our society. Our professionalism as individual psychiatrists inspires trust, one by one, in our patients. Professionalism, moreover, is the foundation of trust for the field of medicine in our society. Our dedication to ensuring that our expertise and motivation are aligned to serve others who are ill, disabled, and suffering is the reason we are given the privilege of being physicians. These ideals are elegant but not always meaningful in the less ethereal, more earthy realms of psychiatric practice. We are invited to create this meaning by translating concepts to practicable behaviors, as we explore in the chapters to come.

Key Points

- *Professionalism* is variously defined but refers to a set of attitudes, skills, and knowledge that defines the professional role of the physician.

- Critics of a "one-size-fits-all" approach to professionalism stress that factors such as economic realities and lifestyle choices must be taken into account in attempts to define it.

- The commercialized nature of healthcare in the United States poses a major threat to professionalism.

- Studies suggest that attention to and concerns regarding professionalism may evolve over the course of training and clinical experience.

- Empirical work suggests that the precepts of professionalism may be supported in principle but ignored in practice.

- Professionalism in psychiatry is more complicated because psychiatrists are held to a higher standard.

- Psychiatry recognizes that the "self" of the psychiatrist can never be completely eliminated from the clinical situation.

- Psychiatry emphasizes that self-reflection and awareness of countertransference are key components of one's professional role.

- Certain professional boundaries involving confidentiality, accepting gifts, and soliciting donations are regarded differently in psychiatry than in the rest of medicine.

Chapter 2

Professionalism and Ethics

From Values to Action

Being a professional is an ethical matter, entailing devotion to a way of life in the service of others and of some higher good.

Leon Kass (1983)

Ethics is an endeavor. It refers to ways of understanding what is good and right in human experience. It is about discernment, knowledge, self-reflection, and it is sustained through seeking, clarifying, translating. It is the concrete expression of moral ideals in everyday life. Ethics is about meaning, and it is about action.

Laura Roberts (2002a)

Professionalism is expressed through ethical action. Noble ideals and abstract principles mean little if they do not guide the daily decisions and behaviors of physicians. In psychiatry, the translation of these humanistic

17

ideals and principles of medicine is found in demonstrations of compassion, in activities that safeguard confidentiality, in the use of expertise to benefit patients, in truthful and fair conduct, and in the willingness to be publicly
accountable for one's work. This is how professionalism is lived in psychiatry—not in mere words, but in the intentional, repeated demonstrations of integrity by psychiatrists whose work is dedicated to improving
the health and circumstances of people with mental illness.

Enacting the ideals and principles of professionalism is, in our view,
especially important in psychiatry. Psychiatrists are like other physicians
in terms of fulfilling the fundamental "promises" of medicine, such as
doing good (beneficence), avoiding harm (nonmaleficence), and being
honest (veracity) and fair (justice), but the professional imperatives of
psychiatry in real life are often greater than those in other specialties of
medicine.

It is not uncommon, for instance, for a surgeon to accept a gift from
a patient who has just undergone a significant operation. The gift should
not be extravagant, and the surgeon should not "expect" a special gift in
order to provide good care to the patient, but it is not unethical by definition for the surgeon to accept this sign of appreciation and gratitude
from a patient. On the other hand, only under the rarest of circumstances
might a psychiatrist ethically accept a gift from a patient, and such an act
would never be without substantive clinical and ethical repercussions.

The heightened responsibilities of psychiatrists derive in part from the
special nature of the kind of suffering that brings someone to seek psychiatric treatment. Mental illnesses are neuropsychiatric conditions that
influence and may distort the thoughts, feelings, behaviors, relationships,
and self-understanding of patients. The specific symptoms of many, although not all, mental illnesses may erode insight and disrupt behaviors.
The chronic nature of many mental illnesses, furthermore, may over time
lead to greater marginalization in society. This means that there will be an
inherent asymmetry in the relationship between psychiatrist and patient,
with one as caregiver and the other as care-seeker, with one as provider
and the other as recipient of care, with one as relatively empowered and
the other relatively disempowered. Because the therapeutic relationship
between psychiatrist and patient is the platform for understanding patients'
illnesses and bringing about healing, psychiatrists are entrusted with approaching this situation of asymmetry with special awareness and a
greater commitment to non-exploitative behavior. Accordingly, psychiatrists' training is unique among the medical specialties in that it formal-

izes and supports rigorous self-reflection; we are required, by the character of our work, to self-observe and understand our role in the therapeutic relationship.

Beyond these reasons, psychiatrists are called on to have greater attentiveness to ethical considerations because of the distinct task we have been given by society in patient care—one in which we are permitted to insist upon or "enforce" treatment against the expressed preferences of our patients under some circumstances. This duty causes us to curtail the liberties of gravely or dangerously ill patients, a responsibility ordinarily carried out only by officers of the law. Indeed, not only are we "permitted" to do so, but we can be held liable for *not* encroaching on what are seen as usual rights of people in these situations.

Finally, because psychiatrists are trained in the dynamics of human interaction, we are often asked to play roles in groups and organizations as leaders, advisors, participants, and consultants. These roles can be far removed from the usual work of mental healthcare but entail informed and ethically sound decision making.

For a psychiatrist, then, professionalism involves—in real time and real action—the ethical application of specialized knowledge and skill to help people living with mental illness and, secondarily, to take certain steps to fulfill responsibilities in society. A psychiatrist enacts professionalism directly and indirectly through clinical care, scientific inquiry, education, disease prevention, health promotion, work with the law, and advocacy. These are sophisticated and nuanced activities, activities that should be undertaken with clarity of thought, rigorous decision making, and careful action. "Intuition" or, more crudely, "gut reactions" are not sufficient for "right action." Right action, as we shall describe, relies on essential professionalism "skills."

Four Essential Professional Skills for Ethical Psychiatric Practice

The ability to render abstract ideals of professionalism into the work of psychiatry is predicated on the sensitivity, attitude, and commitment of the psychiatrist. As noted in Table 2–1, being able to "walk the talk" takes more,

TABLE 2–1. Four essential professional skills for ethical psychiatric practice
Recognizing ethical issues
Appreciating one's own role in the therapeutic process
Anticipating ethically "risky" situations in patient care
Approaching, making, and enacting ethical decisions

however: it takes specific skills (Roberts 1999). These skills involve both knowledge and behaviors and work in concert in fulfilling the goals of sound medical practice.

Skill 1: Recognizing Ethical Issues

The first skill is the capability to recognize ethical considerations arising in the care of patients living with mental illness. Identifying the ethically important features of a clinical case entails attentiveness to underlying motives, beliefs, and values that are present—and may be in tension—in the situation. Being able to see these issues—and to use language that is used and understood by others to describe the issues—is aided by knowledge of the central concepts of biomedical ethics. Many of these terms are defined in Table 2–2 (American Psychiatric Association 2001; Council on Ethical and Judicial Affairs 2002; Jonsen et al. 2002; Roberts and Dyer 2004; Simon 1992).

Sometimes ethical issues in patient care are obvious, and sometimes they are not. Consider the case of Mrs. McGregor.

Mrs. McGregor, a 57-year-old woman, was brought to the emergency department by ambulance in the early morning, unconscious, accompanied by her only son. Physically disabled, she lived alone and took on very limited activities outside her apartment. He had become concerned when he could not reach his mother by telephone the evening before. He drove 150 miles overnight, entering his mother's home to discover that she had indeed taken an overdose of pills. She was breathing deeply but arousable; in transit, she became unconscious. He found a few half-empty bottles, some very old, of prescription tricyclic antidepressant medications and over-the-counter diphenhydramine scattered in the bedroom.

"I knew this would happen. Why did she have to do this again?" he asked. As the patient was stabilized and taken to the intensive care unit,

TABLE 2–2.   **Key biomedical ethics concepts**

Altruism	Acting for the good of others, without self-interest and at times requiring self-sacrifice
Autonomy	Being able to deliberate and make reasoned decisions for one's self and to act on the basis of such decisions; literally "self-rule"
Beneficence	Seeking to bring about good or benefit
Compassion	Literally, "suffering with" another person, with kindness and an active regard for his or her welfare; more closely related to empathy than to sympathy, as the latter connotes the more distanced experience of "feeling sorry for" the individual
Confidentiality	Upholding the obligation not to disclose information obtained from patients or observed about them without their permission; a privilege linked to the legal right of privacy that may at times be overridden by exceptions stipulated in law
Fidelity	Keeping promises, being truthful, and being honorable; in clinical care, the faithfulness with which a clinician commits to the duty of helping patients and acting in a manner that is in keeping with the ideals of the profession
Honesty	Conveying the truth fully, without misrepresentation through deceit, bias, or omission
Integrity	Maintaining professional soundness and reliability of intention and action; a virtue literally defined as wholeness or coherence
Justice	Ensuring fairness; *distributive justice* refers to the fair and equitable distribution of resources and burden through society
Nonmaleficence	Avoiding doing harm
Respect for the law	Acting in accordance with the laws of society

TABLE 2–2.	Key biomedical ethics concepts *(continued)*
Respect for persons	Fully regarding and according intrinsic value to someone or something; reflected in treating another individual with genuine consideration and attentiveness to that person's life history, values, and goals
Voluntarism	Maintaining a belief or acting from one's own free will and ensuring that the belief or action is not coerced or unduly influenced by others

the son explained that she had been "feeling down" for a few weeks. Choked with emotion, he said, "Well, at least it isn't as bad as that one time." He then relayed how his mother had 22 years previously shot herself in the abdomen in an unsuccessful suicide attempt; he had been the first to discover her then as well. She had very severe major depression ("the melancholy kind") and had attempted suicide one other time, roughly 10 years previously.

For two decades, she had lived with severe physical disability and had required repeated abdominal surgeries. In general, when she adhered to her medication regimen, she did well in "managing" her depression, according to the son. "It never quite goes away completely, but she definitely has long stretches where she is very good and I don't worry so much about her."

The son and his wife had been involved in the patient's life, taking her on family outings, to church, and shopping. Four months previously, the son very reluctantly accepted a consulting position in a neighboring town, commuting back and forth to be with his own family and to care for his mother. The son said that both he and his wife felt "terrible, just awful" because they had not checked on his mom as much lately, and they knew that she was losing weight, not caring for herself as well, not interested in visiting as much, and "seeming sad a lot." "We were going to move her to come by us as soon as things settled down," he said.

After the patient was cleared medically, psychiatric hospitalization was recommended. She appeared calm and expressed remorse for having taken the pills. She refused to be admitted to the psychiatric unit, stating that she would take medications but she did not want to be in the hospital. She stated that she was not suicidal but acknowledged that she had had "several rough months" in which dying seemed an inviting "release" from the pain of her life. The patient's cognition was excellent, and there was no indication of psychosis. She did appear "flat" and withdrawn. She said, "Don't tell my son about all of this. He has a lot to worry about, with the boys and a new job. I will be fine."

The son and daughter-in-law said that they could arrange to move the patient to their new neighborhood but needed a couple of weeks to put it all together. "And I'm scared she'll do it again. I've seen this whole deal before. She seems fine, and she isn't."

The need to hospitalize a desperately ill woman with melancholic depression and a recent suicide attempt clearly presents a number of ethically important considerations. On one hand, it is important to respect the personal rights and preferences of the patient regarding her care, especially one who seems calm and expresses willingness to accept recommended medications. On the other hand, the psychiatrist has several ethical duties in this situation that do not permit strict adherence to the stated preferences of the patient. The physician first must endeavor to improve the health of the patient who is affected by a treatable illness. The physician should also act to prevent potentially life-threatening harm that may occur if the illness progresses without intervention. A further duty is to live up to legal imperatives associated with the physician's role in protecting individuals who are endangered by virtue of their mental illnesses. In the case of Mrs. McGregor, there are further complexities regarding protecting the privacy of the patient. From the point of view of the caregivers, her son has been involved in her care and has shown himself to be conscientious, positive, and loving. She appears to appreciate his involvement and help, and yet after the acute medical crisis has resolved, she wants her son to know fewer details about her health condition. More rigorous boundaries related to the patient's wish for privacy have to come into play as her wishes become more clearly expressed and her care transitions from one set of care providers to another.

In the language of ethics, this situation represents a complex interaction of the principles of autonomy ("self-governance"), beneficence (the "positive" duty to do good), and nonmaleficence (the "negative" duty to avoid harm) and the duty to fulfill expectations in the eyes of the law (i.e., respect for the law). Psychiatrists are entrusted with the special responsibility of placing gravely or dangerously ill people on "holds," curtailing their freedoms, and implementing involuntary treatment in order to ensure patient safety and well-being. It is a dramatic experience to take away the liberty of another human being, and there are constraints on when it may be undertaken. For instance, it must be performed in a manner that is "least restrictive"—that is, a patient should not be kept in a locked unit if an unlocked unit or a day treatment setting will suffice, a patient should be cared for nearer to home than farther away from home, if possible, and a patient should not be hospitalized at all if an ambulatory clinic setting will suffice.

The privilege of confidentiality (i.e., the physician's responsibility to not disclose personal information or observations about a patient without the patient's permission) also evolves in this particular case. Initially, when she is unconscious, the imperative to intervene to save her life allows the medical care team to speak relatively freely with the patient's family as well as to take steps medically, even though she is unable to give informed consent. This is referred to as "presumed consent" or "emergency consent." As the patient becomes more alert, and it becomes clear that she is "more intact," her abilities to express preferences regarding her care and her privacy are also incrementally restored. This case scenario is interesting in that Mrs. McGregor's capacity to direct her care is still apparently diminished, whereas her capacity to direct how her privacy is protected in relation to her family may be more fully in place. The emergency department physicians, the intensive care unit physicians, and the psychiatric physicians thus encounter different tensions regarding patient beneficence, nonmaleficence, autonomy, and confidentiality.

Such complex and subtle ethical issues arise in other patient care situations. One example pertains to the confidentiality concerns and personal, cultural, and religious values that may emerge in talking with patients about their intimate relationships and sexual health while clarifying symptoms and establishing a diagnosis. Similarly, what is ethically important about how one documents a "VIP" patient's history, current substance use pattern, or psychotherapy session in an electronic medical record? How does the psychiatrist balance, on one hand, the need to communicate accurate information to other healthcare professionals who may be involved in the patient's care with, on the other hand, the need to take steps to avoid damage that could occur if there were a breach of the patient's confidentiality?

Another illustration is the careful process of discussing risks, benefits, and alternatives and a patient's life goals when seeking consent for a newly recommended treatment. Preserving appropriate confidentiality lines with a patient's family members can be very difficult, especially at certain points in the treatment process when giving some details on general topics but none on sensitive issues can be just as revealing as overt disclosures. Even more nuanced are the ethics issues that arise, for instance, in harmonizing a patient's expectations regarding frequency of appointments with the realities of scheduling in a busy outpatient clinic or in establishing "ground rules" for psychotherapy when a patient works in the same setting as a caregiving psychiatrist. A conscientious professional is cognizant of, and attentive to, how these everyday activities are ethically meaningful.

Skill 2: Appreciating One's Own Role in the Therapeutic Process

A second essential ethics skill relates to the psychiatrist's ability to reflect on the treatment relationship and to appreciate how his or her manner, attitudes, past experiences, skill set, and individual approach may influence the nature and course of the therapeutic process (Roberts and Dyer 2004). Because so much of psychiatric training focuses on this ability to self-observe and self-appraise, psychiatrists are well positioned to enact this second vital ethics skill (Roberts 2003; Roberts and Dyer 2004).

Thinking about one's role in the therapeutic process is second nature for experienced and talented psychiatrists; nevertheless, thinking through the ethical considerations may require some extra effort. Consider the example of a psychiatrist who is interacting with the worried mother of an older adolescent patient and may experience the natural desire to reassure the mother that her son is not engaged in sexual activity. Disclosing this information without his explicit permission may change the therapeutic boundaries established at the beginning of treatment, and, importantly, in many states such a disclosure is essentially breaking the law. The psychiatrist may feel the emotional pull to alleviate the mother's anxieties. This may be particularly strong when the psychiatrist has concerns about his own teenage children or if he has other reasons to identify with or want to "please" the patient's mother. Moreover, what happens if the patient does indeed begin a sexual relationship in a few months' time? The seemingly benign reassurance "now" may set up a much more complicated dynamic in the future when questions are met, perhaps, with silence rather than reassurance. One's own desire to be a "good guy" in the eyes of the patient's mother, or other motivation that causes the psychiatrist to deviate from usual therapeutic practices, can jeopardize the ethical framework of the patient's care, including appropriate privacy boundaries, as well as create new dilemmas related to the professionalism of the psychiatrist. A psychiatrist will need to recognize these ethically relevant issues in the clinical situation and assess his or her own "participation" in the ethical dynamics that exist.

Recognizing one's strengths and weaknesses as a psychiatrist is also important from an ethical perspective. This may include a psychiatrist's recognized expertise in working with people with certain health conditions, with very seriously ill patients, or with patients with complex medical-psychiatric co-occurring conditions. On the other hand, knowing one's weaknesses, such as discomfort in working with certain "difficult" patients, can be very helpful in optimizing patient care practices by professionals. Even harder, however, is sorting out situations in which one really enjoys working with patients that make one feel "special" but doing so may create greater ethical vulnerabilities. A psychiatrist may experience greater temptation to "rescue" a patient with an addiction, for instance, when that is a role the psychiatrist played in his own family in the past. Similarly, a psychiatrist may feel a greater temptation to make quiet mention or to allude to the care of a "VIP" patient in work or personal settings because of the sense of stature that comes with the role of psychiatrist in this situation.

A related notion is the ethical imperative to work within one's areas of clinical competence ("scope of practice"), except under rare and unexpected circumstances. The most obvious example is an emergency situation in which, in the absence of others with greater expertise, a physician must try to do what he or she can. In rural and frontier settings with clinician/ specialist shortages, however, psychiatrists are often called on to stretch the limits of their knowledge and skill. Efforts to expand one's overall competence by working with specialists elsewhere, building a multidisciplinary team, or seeking additional training is important ethically as well as clinically in these difficult situations.

This skill involves paying attention to one's thoughts, feelings, and reactions and to the limits of one's knowledge. It thus involves a sophisticated attunement to countertransference in the therapeutic situation as well as self-honesty in appraising one's preparation and knowledge for the specific clinical issues in the case. The clinician's sense of anxiety about a case—the sense of being in "deep waters," of being "in over one's head"—and other emotional markers, such as the pull to "rescue," to worry excessively, or to become overly excited or overly involved, are all important from both clinical and ethical perspectives. These are natural experiences for a clinician who is working with multiproblem, complex people with mental illnesses, and less-seasoned psychiatrists may not recognize these insights and impulses as gifts that may help inform the therapeutic process and help the clinician steer clear of ethical transgressions and poor clinical decisions, if recognized for their value (Roberts 2003; Roberts and Dyer 2004).

Nevertheless, it may be hard for some to see how one's personal "style," biases, blind spots, or lack of sufficient expertise may negatively affect patient care, so it is important for psychiatrists—as with other health professionals—to make intentional efforts to enhance this skill. This is particularly true in light of the potential vulnerabilities of people with diverse mental illnesses; these conditions, by definition, intermittently or progressively affect a person's feelings, sense of self and insight, perceptions, ideas, ability to arrange one's thoughts and make decisions, energy level, motivation, behavior, psychological development over time, and ultimately ability to develop and preserve healthy relationships and to contribute in society. Certain mental illnesses may interfere with the ability to advocate for oneself (Roberts 2002b), and mental illnesses have significant mortality and morbidity due to direct physical disease burden and the burden associated with co-occurring illnesses (World Health Organization Department of Mental Health and Substance Abuse 2006). Thus, working therapeutically with patients who are living with diseases that may so profoundly shape their life experience creates a heightened ethical imperative to be self-aware in their care (Roberts 1999).

Indeed, the capacity to monitor one's personal impact in the therapeutic process is especially important from an ethical perspective because it helps to minimize harm to patients. In an extreme example, the "lovesick" psychiatrist who is unaware of his personal need for emotional sustenance may begin to distort the therapeutic process toward self-gratification rather than serving the well-being of the patient through rigorous adherence to correct professional behaviors (Epstein et al. 1992; Gabbard 1999; Gabbard and Lester 2003). A less extreme example—but one in which there is the potential for significant harm—is the psychiatrist who is best prepared to provide psychopharmacological treatment and gives disproportionate emphasis to this therapeutic approach, even when caring for patients for whom psychosocial treatments may be more appropriate or beneficial. More positively, a psychiatrist who understands his or her strengths in working with certain conditions or psychological issues can harness these qualities to bring about better outcomes for patients as well as live up to professionalism expectations in these clinical care situations.

Skill 3: Anticipating Ethically "Risky" Situations in Patient Care

Not unlike other specialties of medicine, psychiatry is rich with ethical meaning but also riddled with ethical risks. Certain features of mental illness and its treatment give rise to especially problematic ethical ("high-risk") situations that, in turn, increase the "stakes" for the psychiatrist. Suicide and grave passive neglect, for instance, accompany many mood, psychotic, cognitive, and substance-related disorders. Similarly, impulsivity, eroded judgment, and behavioral disruption associated with mental illness may place innocent others and society in danger. Consequently, the psychiatrist, by virtue of his or her clinical role and legal responsibilities, may be required to intervene intensively to ensure the safety of his or her patients and others around them. The psychiatrist thus may be in a situation, for instance, in which he or she must disclose personal information about the patient to authorities (e.g., the courts, child protective services, the police) or to others who are at risk of being hurt (e.g., explicitly named, intended victims of violence, family members). It is important to note that this action is in accord with professionalism standards. Disclosure of patient information, when mandated, is not technically a "violation" of confidentiality, because it is not a right (as privacy is, in the United States) but instead a privilege accorded by society—a privilege that may be suspended from time to time, as in the descriptions here. There are many possible ethical errors in such situations, including waiting too long or being too quick in the disclosure process, underestimating risk due to lack of sufficient information, or having new challenges in the therapeutic relationship when the psychiatrist must assume a role that is experienced as adversarial by the patient.

Psychiatrists in certain settings and with certain kinds of subspecialty expertise may be more likely to encounter certain types of ethically risky patient care situations. The psychiatrist in the busy emergency department will deal with issues related to self-harm, dangerousness, and involuntary treatment, bringing autonomy, beneficence, confidentiality, and related ethical issues to the fore. The consultation-liaison psychiatrist will deal with end-of-life care issues, raising difficult concerns related to autonomy, compassion, beneficence, and nonmaleficence. The rural psychiatrist may encounter clinical issues of great complexity that stretch beyond local resources or subspecialty expertise, causing him or her to work at the edges of clinical competence. The child psychiatrist will deal with concerns about abuse and neglect of young people, leading to significant interventions and mandatory reporting requirements. The psychiatrist with addictions expertise will treat patients with diverse behaviors and often legal issues that lead to dual roles, with their accompanying ethical challenges.

The professionalism issue to be considered here is the observation that psychiatrists are highly likely to encounter these issues—issues that can be properly understood as problematic from an ethical perspective and that will challenge the clarity of their thinking, their wisdom in facing uncertainty and complexity, and their integrity. Stated another way, psychiatric care can generate ethical "risk" because psychiatrists are entrusted with using their special expertise and their societally defined power in a manner that may impinge upon traditions, expectations, and the usual rights of individuals who are mentally ill (American Psychiatric Association 2001; Roberts and Dyer 2004; Simon 1992). For these reasons, it is important that psychiatrists become skillful in anticipating when the care of certain patients may produce these difficult situations and be prepared to handle them responsibly and safely, according to the expectations of the profession.

Skill 4: Approaching, Making, and Enacting Ethical Decisions

The psychiatrist who is cognizant of clinical ethical issues, observes accurately his or her own role in the therapeutic process, and anticipates potential conflicts is well positioned for approaching, making, and enacting ethical decisions (Roberts and Dyer 2004). An initial step is thorough and careful data gathering about a patient case. Many apparently "ethical" issues (e.g., related to a patient's preferences or a difference of opinion among family members regarding treatment options) quickly resolve once background information is obtained and sorted out. Linked to this is the need to determine whether it would be valuable to obtain additional expertise, including the appropriate use of consultants (e.g., clinical, legal, and/or ethical specialists) or the involvement of trusted supervisors. Including the perspectives of "wise persons" is particularly helpful when dealing with a "difficult" patient who presents a "high-risk" ethical situation. Written resources such as codes of ethics, policy documents, the conceptual literature, and the evidence-based ethics studies may also be of assistance in this initial data-gathering phase.

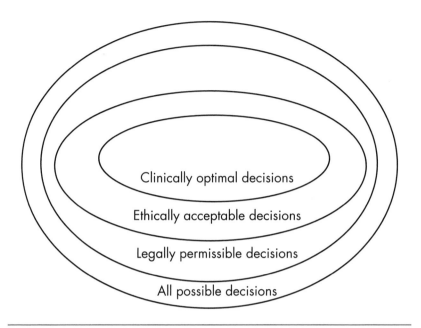

FIGURE 2–1.   **The relationship of legally permissible, ethically acceptable, and clinically optimal decisions in psychiatric patient care.**

Once the clinician is more fully informed, a next step is undertaking an explicit, careful process of ethical decision making. In many instances, a formal ethical decision-making model may be of help in illuminating, evaluating, and selecting a wise course of action in an ethically complex situation.

As illustrated in Figure 2–1, it is essential to recognize the full set of possible options (including no action at all), to learn what is legally permissible under the circumstances, to think through different possibilities that may be ethically acceptable, and finally to decide upon an optimal approach to the clinical care of the patient.

Jonsen et al. (2002) proposed a sequential clinical ethics decision-making model relying on the ethical principles of fidelity, beneficence, clinical competence, and nonmaleficence. This model highlights four components, in order of relative importance: 1) clinical indications; 2) preferences of patients; 3) quality of life; and 4) socioeconomic or external factors. This approach is viewed as "patient-centered" rather than focused on broader societal issues, and it is strongly driven by standards of care and clinical best practices. The application of this model is illustrated in Figure 2–2.

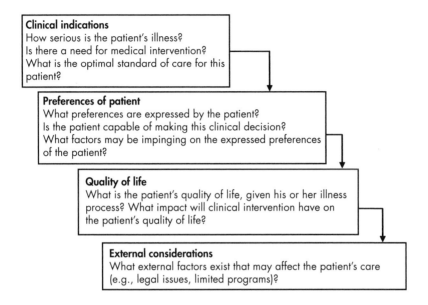

Clinical indications
How serious is the patient's illness?
Is there a need for medical intervention?
What is the optimal standard of care for this patient?

Preferences of patient
What preferences are expressed by the patient?
Is the patient capable of making this clinical decision?
What factors may be impinging on the expressed preferences of the patient?

Quality of life
What is the patient's quality of life, given his or her illness process? What impact will clinical intervention have on the patient's quality of life?

External considerations
What external factors exist that may affect the patient's care (e.g., legal issues, limited programs)?

FIGURE 2–2. Clinical ethics decision-making model.
Source. Reprinted from Roberts LW, Dyer AR (eds): "Health Care Ethics Committees," in *Concise Guide to Ethics in Mental Health Care.* Washington, DC, American Psychiatric Publishing, 2004, p. 307. Used with permission.

Mrs. Bloughen was in the midst of a severe asthma attack and was brought to an urgent-care facility by a neighbor. Her condition rapidly deteriorated, and she was transferred to an emergency department. There Mrs. Bloughen refused intubation, indicating that she wished to die and that this was her "right." She was panicked and distraught but adamant. Past records indicated that Mrs. Bloughen had a history of borderline personality disorder, drank heavily, and struggled each day with feelings of despair and anger. According to the neighbor, Mrs. Bloughen had lost her family, her job, and "all her friends but me" over the previous 5 years. The neighbor said that Mrs. Bloughen often would say that she looked upon dying with "no fear whatsoever" and "the sooner the better."

In this case, there are formidable tensions between the principles of beneficence (i.e., providing emergency treatment in order to save her life) and autonomy (i.e., the stated preference to die). The clinical ethics model resolves this apparently irresolvable problem, however, through the following logic. Intervention is clinically indicated and is likely to bring benefit. It is the appropriate standard of care in essentially all emergency contexts in the United States, and it is the expectation and duty of a physician to respond in this manner. In addition, there are reasons to believe that the patient has significant illness processes (i.e., preexisting depression with suicidality and acute distress and discomfort) that may be distorting her ability to formulate and/or to express sustained, authentic wishes. Moreover, the consequences of not intervening are grave, and failure to act will bring about irreversible harm. This approach is not meant to diminish the autonomy of the individual but rather acknowledges that there may be forces at play that are already interfering with her genuine autonomy (Roberts 2003).

This decision-making approach places clinical considerations first, with the rationale that the wise and respectful application of clinical expertise to benefit patients is the physician's foremost responsibility and helps prevent irreversible harm. It is often "conservative" in that it allows most often for preservation of life and enhanced quality of life through clinical intervention. This decision-making approach thus deeply combines clinical and ethical imperatives in arriving at "solutions" to ethical "problems."

In addition to this clinical ethics approach, a widely accepted but conceptually focused bioethics decision-making model was developed by the moral philosophers Beauchamp and Childress (2001); it gives primacy to the cardinal ethics principles of beneficence, autonomy, nonmaleficence, and justice. The methodology for decision making, in short, is to think through how these principles relate to the patient case, from which emerges greater conceptual clarity about a recommended course of action. In a similar approach, Hundert (1987) suggested a strategy in which "hidden" conflicts in values are identified and resolved by being made explicit, then further clarified and prioritized.

Finally, beyond these models for decision making that pertain to all ethical aspects of patient care, Drane (1984) proposed a special model related to ethical and legal standards for decisional capacity and informed decision making. In what has been characterized as a "sliding scale" methodology, higher-risk decisions (e.g., informed consent or informed refusal) require that patients possess higher levels of decisional capacity and participate in more rigorous consent processes. On the other hand, decisions that may be viewed as lower risk are not as "demanding" ethically (Roberts and Dyer 2004). Stated differently, lower-risk decisions involve less rigorous standards for decisional capacity and consent processes.

To illustrate this approach, because of the potential risks involved, a patient living with a severe and persistent mental illness who demands discharge from the hospital while still experiencing suicidal ideation must meet a very high standard for informed refusal of care and must participate in very rigorous informed consent/refusal procedures before being permitted to leave against medical advice would even be considered by a conscientious clinician. A less rigorous standard is needed, however, when a patient is considering whether to have a flu shot, a cholesterol check, or even a medication serum level checked, under most circumstances.

A last step in approaching, making, and enacting ethical decisions is ensuring that there are appropriate safeguards in place to help support, or correct quickly, a decision that is implemented in an ethically difficult patient care situation (Roberts and Dyer 2004; Simon 1992). Safeguards are diverse and their appropriateness is dependent on the issues at hand. Safeguards may include advance directives, careful treatment planning performed in collaboration with a well-informed patient, inclusion of alternative decision makers or court-ordered guardians, disclosure of potential conflicts of interest, documentation of decision sequences, introduction of additional confidentiality protections, discussion with consultants or ethics committee members, treatment team education around complicated patient care issues, and adequate follow-up arrangements for treatment.

Values to Action: Using Professional Skills in Clinical Psychiatry

A psychiatrist is a professional who is entrusted with serving others in meaningful, practical ways. Thus, the psychiatrist must not only wish to be good, so to speak, but also endeavor to do good through professional work. We suggest that attaining these aims relies on four professional skills. Fortunately, psychiatric training fosters these ethical as well as clinical skills, including cultivating sensitivity, self-awareness, expertise, and explicit problem-solving and valuing supervision and consultation. This said, the practice of psychiatry gives rise to ethically as well as clinically complex patient care situations. For these reasons, we believe that psychiatrists may be very well prepared for the ethical aspects of their work but also, correctly, will be held to the highest standards of professional conduct.

Key Points

- Psychiatrists may have heightened awareness of ethics consideration and professionalism because of their unique training in the dynamics of human interaction, societal responsibilities, and the power differential of the doctor-patient relationship during the treatment of a patient with mental illness.

- The four essential professional skills for ethical psychiatric practice are recognizing ethical issues, appreciating one's own role in the therapeutic process, anticipating ethically "risky" situations in psychiatric care, and approaching, making, and enacting ethical decisions.

- A psychiatrist must be able to identify the interplay of ethical issues while fulfilling legal responsibilities.

- The capacity to recognize both the scope of one's clinical competence and the limits of one's personal capacities are essential professional skills in minimizing harm to patients.

- Psychiatrists in certain care settings and subspecialties should be prepared to handle ethically risky patient care situations involving issues related to self-harm, dangerousness, and involuntary treatment. These situations affect specific ethics principles, such as beneficence, confidentiality, and the patient's autonomy.

- Several models have been developed to assist psychiatric clinicians when evaluating a risky ethical situation. These include the "patient centered" sequential ethics decision-making model, the bioethics decision-making model, and the ethical and legal standards for decisional capacity.

- Appropriate safeguards should be established once a decision is made in difficult patient care situations.

Chapter 3

Professionalism and the Clinical Relationship

Boundaries and Beyond

In Chapter 1 we noted that psychiatrists are held to a higher standard in many areas of professionalism, particularly when it comes to boundaries in the doctor-patient relationship. The idea that psychiatrists must be "more ethical" than other physicians has been the subject of considerable controversy, and yet it has a definite rationale. Of all medical specialties, psychiatry pays singular attention to the relationship as a core feature of the therapeutic action. The psychological subtext of every interaction between psychiatrist and patient is clinically important because of its unique and powerful role in the healing process. Moreover, it is ethically important because it involves understanding and working directly with the most sensitive and intimate aspects of the patient's life.

The heightened role of professionalism is most apparent in the context of psychotherapy. Transference is carefully observed and discussed. Countertransference is examined under a microscope to see what it reveals about both doctor and patient. The relationship between psychotherapist and patient is viewed as a laboratory in which the patient's relationship difficulties can be studied *in statu nascendi* as they emerge in the transference. The nature of this deeper connection between psychotherapist and patient as fundamental to adducing greater health and well-being in the patient often means that the psychotherapist assumes a substantive and influential role in the patient's life. Consider the contrast with the relationship with a dermatologist who, although knowing the patient's history, literally works more superficially to recognize and treat lesions of the skin. The potential for exploitation is greater in psychiatry than in many other specialties and, for this reason, the professionalism requirements of our field are also greater if we are to fulfill the companion imperatives of doing good and avoiding harm.

Although professional boundaries are particularly important in psychotherapy, it would be a mistake to conclude that other activities of a psychiatrist involve a different set of boundaries. Psychotherapy is a basic "science" of psychiatry, and the principles of psychotherapeutic management are also involved in evaluation, consultation, pharmacotherapy, and other aspects of clinical management performed in the routine activities of psychiatrists . The power differential in the patient's transference to the doctor is not created by the practice of psychotherapy. It is integral to the fact that whenever a psychiatrist sees a patient, a *fiduciary relationship* is established—that is, the patient entrusts his or her welfare to a professional who possesses specific expertise and is ethically obligated to provide a service that advances the well-being and interests of the patient (Gabbard and Nadelson 1995). The sensitivity of the "data" that psychiatrists gather and employ in the care of the patient and the potential vulnerability of the patient as he or she comes to the attention of a psychiatrist, taken together, again affirm the special professionalism responsibilities of psychiatrists in clinical endeavors outside of formal psychotherapy.

Defining Boundaries

Professional boundaries constitute an envelope within which the doctor-patient relationship can thrive and the patient's well-being is supported as the sole focus of clinical interactions. The initial task, of course, is learning what the patient's concern is and identifying the nature of the problems that brought the patient to psychiatric attention. Understanding and developing a therapeutic approach to the patient is essential, and addressing the patient's true needs is paramount. Boundaries therefore represent

TABLE 3–1.	Examples of behaviors upholding professional boundaries in psychiatry

Absence of any form of sexual contact

Limited physical contact of any kind

Consistent and appropriate timing, length, and location
of sessions

Respectful language and style of communication

Suitable attire

Judicious use of self-disclosure

Appropriate efforts to protect patient privacy and to uphold
the privilege of confidentiality

Abstinence from business transactions other than the fee
for service

Limitations on gifts to or from patient

a set of professional behaviors that establish a predictable, constructive treatment context for the patient, but professional boundaries also create optimal conditions for the doctor to function, building a frame that is helpful in fulfilling his or her responsibilities to the patient and making clinical errors and ethical mistakes less likely to occur.

Table 3–1 summarizes several examples of the professional boundary considerations that all psychiatrists must take into account when they see a patient. Together, these become a set of defining features that constitute the envelope within which diagnosis and treatment take place.

The absence of sexual contact has primacy in the set of behaviors that represent therapeutic boundaries and is an "absolute" in professional conduct by psychiatrists. The unfortunate frequency with which sexual exploitation of patients occurs has been largely responsible for the emphasis on professional boundaries in recent decades. However, sexual boundary violations are not as common as nonsexual forms of transgressions, and it is also true that in most cases, the sexual relationship with a patient is preceded by a "slippery slope" characterized by a progressive series of nonsexual boundary violations (Gabbard 2008; Gutheil and Gabbard 1993; Strasburger et al. 1992). Hence, the monitoring of small shifts in the professional boundaries is a way of preventing more egregious breaches of the therapeutic relationship.

Professional Role

An overarching concept when thinking about boundaries is the unique aspects of the role when one is functioning as a professional with a patient. The psychiatrist is not a friend, a sibling, a parent, a lover, or a business associate. The psychiatrist's job is to listen carefully to the patient's story and come up with an accurate diagnosis and an optimal treatment plan. All of the psychiatrist's activities and everything the psychiatrist says must be grounded in the professional understanding of why the two parties are there: to diagnose or treat the patient.

Professional roles can sometimes be misconstrued as involving excessive rigidity or formality. Forming a solid therapeutic alliance and establishing rapport requires warmth and empathy. The patient must also see that there is some degree of flexibility in the professional's demeanor. Although it is professional and respectful to begin a first meeting with "Ms. Smith" or "Mr. Jones," one is not absolutely required to refer to the patient in this formal manner. Some patients insist on being called by their first name because it makes them feel more relaxed and comfortable, and the psychiatrist may need to adjust by acceding to the patient's request to be called by first name. On the other hand, under most circumstances, the clinician is referred to by title (i.e., Dr. Smith as opposed to "Mary" or "Charlie"), and this helps to keep perspective on the expertise of the physician who has assumed responsibility for caring for the patient. Still, in certain situations, such as in a small community setting or some forms of therapy it can come across as rather authoritarian, superior, or demanding if the psychiatrist insists on being called "Doctor," when the patient prefers to be called by his or her first name. In fact, in therapy it is often a good policy to simply let patients call the doctor whatever they wish (within reason) and then explore the reasons for their choice.

Confidentiality

In psychiatric practice, confidentiality is the professional obligation to protect the patient by not disclosing aspects of his or her thoughts, feelings, and personal history without the patient's explicit permission. There are exceptions to this obligation, such as when a patient is a clear and immediate threat toward others or when the possibility of sexual, physical, or emotional abuse of a vulnerable individual is at stake, and for this reason it is considered a "privilege" rather than a "right." Privacy, on the other hand, is understood to be more fundamental: the historical right of an individual to keep his or her thoughts, feelings, body, and details of his or her personal history separate and free from unwanted or uninvited intrusion. Safeguarding patient confidentiality is a cardinal professional boundary, and it is mandated by federal laws, such as the Health Insurance Portability and Accountability Act of 1996, for all physicians.

The stigma associated with seeing a psychiatrist and the sharing of excruciatingly painful thoughts, feelings, and behaviors require an atmosphere of unequivocal confidentiality. When first entering the field of psychiatry, trainees and practitioners may have some difficulty recognizing the pervasive and profound nature of the behavioral constraints stemming from confidentiality:

- Psychiatrists cannot acknowledge whether they treat a particular patient.
- Psychiatrists must be cautious of using the patient's name when greeting the patient in the waiting room.
- Psychiatrists cannot repeat information they hear during a psychiatric appointment, nor can they act on any information that is revealed (a classic example is the stock market tip).
- The ethical demands of psychiatric confidentiality require the psychiatrist to be deceptive on certain occasions.

A clinical illustration may flesh out some of these concerns.

Dr. Blakely, a psychiatrist in an academic medical center, received a call from Dr. Miller, an associate dean for research at the medical school, who felt he was getting depressed and could not function efficiently. Dr. Blakely consented to see him because he had no outside contact with him or with research. In fact, he hardly knew Dr. Miller. At the first appointment, Dr. Miller said he was deeply concerned about confidentiality because he did not want colleagues at the medical center to know that he was seeing a psychiatrist. He asked if he would be placed in the electronic medical record. Dr. Blakely said he could keep a handwritten record and create a chart that would be locked in his desk rather than in the computerized medical record that was generally used within the medical center. Dr. Miller then revealed that he and his wife had decided to get a divorce. Dr. Blakely had met Dr. Miller's wife because she was a hematologist who had consulted him once about a patient. After evaluating Dr. Miller for 50 minutes, Dr. Blakely told Dr. Miller that he had some symptoms of depression, but not enough to make the diagnosis, and that psychotherapy might be the most useful course of treatment at the moment. He did not think medication was indicated. Dr. Miller agreed to the treatment plan, and they made an appointment for the following week.

As Dr. Miller left Dr. Blakely's office, a psychiatric resident arrived early for supervision with Dr. Blakely. When he came into supervision, without thinking he said to Dr. Blakely, "What on earth is Dr. Miller doing over here?" Dr. Blakely was in a dilemma. If he said that he could not speak about it or it was confidential, it might be an indirect acknowledgement that he was treating him. If he said nothing, there could also be an embarrassing moment where he would be revealing something about the nature of the visit. He decided to compromise by simply responding with, "It's a long story." In this way, he did not acknowledge whether Dr. Miller was a patient, nor did he reveal anything confidential. He then immediately changed the subject and asked his supervisee which patient he would like to discuss that day.

As Dr. Blakely left his office at the end of the day, he got on the elevator with a psychiatrist colleague in his department who worked on a different floor. Only the two of them were in the elevator, and the colleague said, "Did you hear that Miller is leaving his wife?" Again, Dr. Blakely had to think quickly about what he could say. He had learned the information only through the clinical contact with Dr. Miller, so he could not acknowledge that he knew it. If he *had* heard it from a nonconfidential source, then of course he would be free to say that he was aware of it. Having anticipated this situation might arise, he was prepared and responded, "Really?" His colleague just said, "That's what I heard today."

In the elevator incident, Dr. Blakely struggled with how to respond. It appears that he had two ethical imperatives in conflict: the duty to be honest and the duty to safeguard the patient's confidentiality. He opted to say something that was true ("It is a long story") and yet obscured certain aspects of the situation in order to protect the patient. One might argue that this is somewhat deceptive, subordinating complete honesty in the interest of a higher ethical principle of confidentiality. He was not comfortable with his blank-faced response, but he had to maintain the confidentiality of the doctor-patient relationship with the associate dean, even though it meant not telling "the whole truth" in the response to his colleague. Moreover, he was faced with a challenge in treating the associate dean because he would have to compartmentalize certain information that would come up in the course of the treatment because he had heard it only from a patient. Thus he had to work diligently to keep in mind what he had heard from Dr. Miller versus what he had heard from other sources. This challenge to compartmentalize is particularly difficult when one treats colleagues. Moreover, when Dr. Blakely arrived home for the evening, he was a bit distressed at the news of the divorce, and he felt like ventilating with his wife about it, but he knew he was bound by an ethical principle that kept him from doing so. Practically speaking, if he let out anything he had heard to his wife, and she let on that she knew about the impending divorce, there was a risk that it would get back to the associate dean and he would feel betrayed. Hence Dr. Blakely had to struggle with the information by himself, containing it, processing it, and mulling it over throughout the evening.

Dr. Blakely did have one recourse that was entirely ethical: he could seek out formal consultation with a professional colleague, especially one from another city who would not know the people involved. Seeking consultation has all the confidentiality of psychotherapy, and the name of the patient does not need to be revealed, so the identity of the patient can be at least partially protected.

Other dilemmas present themselves with confidentiality as well. The gossiping psychiatrist is not a rarity. One often hears information that one is dying to tell a friend or colleague because of the "specialness" of being the keeper of secrets. Celebrity patients also may tempt some to breach confidentiality. The temptation to share with others must be resisted—it is about the gratification of the clinician and does not support the well-being of the patient whatsoever. Moreover, the psychiatrist who breaches confidentiality is short sighted and unwise as well as unprofessional because it undermines his or her reputation and credibility among others—even among the people who seem "hungriest" for the most recent gossip—and it creates vulnerability to a lawsuit or a sanction from a professional organization or licensing board in the future.

Case material must be used in the process of teaching and learning. The ethical requirements of confidentiality are often at odds with the needs of education. Psychiatric residents who present a case in a seminar must be careful to disguise certain features of the patient so that the person is not recognizable to someone in the seminar. However, even disguise does not assure that the patient may not be known by someone, so any listener who thinks he or she might know the patient being presented is ethically bound to leave the room.

The same concern, of course, applies to a psychiatrist or a resident who wishes to write up a case for publication. Considerable controversy exists regarding whether one should obtain permission from the patient before disguising the case and presenting it or publishing it (Gabbard 2000; Kantrowitz 2006). Some have argued that introducing consent into the clinical process can disrupt it because of the psychiatrist's needs taking precedence over the patient's needs. Moreover, patients may feel they *must* grant consent because they do not want to displease the psychiatrist, even though they have serious reservations. On the other hand, there are cases in which patients have *not* been asked permission to publish and then inadvertently discover a published account of themselves. Such patients may feel violated and betrayed (Gabbard 2000). The discussion of this issue amongst ethicists is interesting in that it has historically been permissible to "deceive" by intentionally withholding, distorting, or altering information to protect patient confidentiality but *only* if the clinical "teaching value" of the case is not undermined by the deception and the fact that information has been changed is acknowledged explicitly (i.e., the deception is disclosed and dealt with honestly). In recent years, however, ethicists have moved toward the position of an emerging standard that consent must be obtained if it is feasible.

If an author chooses to disguise patient data in a case write-up, one must be careful to protect the patient's identity while not altering the clinical data in such a way that it would be misleading to the reader. For example, if a patient with depression is changed to bulimia, or a patient who has been given electroconvulsive therapy is described as having deep brain stimulation, the clinical implications of the case will be dramatically different in terms of the reader's understanding of the clinical significance of the report.

One cannot overemphasize the importance of confidentiality. Without the assurance that information stays in the room, many patients will be reluctant to share the pieces of their lives with the greatest meaning, whether they be stories of vulnerability and intimacy or their worst fears and darkest secrets. The psychiatrist then will have only partial information, which may distort, disturb, and prolong the process of helping the patient to attain therapeutic aims of the work.

Confidentiality is not absolute, of course, and in all states there are some exceptions. Psychiatrists may need to explain these exceptions to their patients so that they understand the doctor's obligations. For example, in every state of the country one must break confidentiality to report instances of child abuse. In some states, suspected emotional or physical mistreatment of a dependent elder triggers mandatory reporting to local officials. More commonly, if the patient is deemed lethally suicidal, the psychiatrist may need to call a family member to assure safety or to commit the patient to a hospital. Technically, these are not "breaches" of the privilege of confidentiality in the way that revealing patient information in casual conversation is a breach, because there is a professional obligation (i.e., to adhere to the law) that "trumps" the obligation to protect sensitive patient information. If a psychiatrist is contemplating a breach of confidentiality for reasons that are not clearly dictated by law, however, it is advisable that he or she check with a knowledgeable colleague or even an attorney before making a misstep.

Time and Place

Psychiatrists largely make a living by selling their time, and they must divide their appointments into reasonable intervals, such as 20–30 minutes for a medication appointment or 45–50 minutes for psychotherapy. Sometimes 90 minutes will be necessary for the initial evaluation. Time is also a boundary that allows the psychiatrist to have an organized schedule that facilitates consistency in the doctor-patient relationship. If one extends sessions for a single patient, the entire schedule can become off-kilter for the rest of the day and lead to feelings on the part of other patients that their time pressures and needs are not respected. The time constraints should be explained early on to each patient so there is an expectation that when the session is over, the patient must leave. There are occasional exceptions made when someone is hysterically sobbing or otherwise distressed in such a way as to cause the clinician to worry about suicide or psychotic decompensation. As a matter of course, however, patients must be told that their session must end at the appointed time because it would be inconsiderate of the next patient, and the clinician may need to remind them of this periodically.

The location of the appointment is usually in an office or a hospital unit. There are, of course, variations based on the individualized treatment plan. A patient with an elevator phobia may need to be taken to a tall building and given in vivo exposure by riding up and down the elevator in the company of the therapist. This form of behavior therapy is well established and effective, and the clinician can document the need for a different treatment setting in the patient's medical record. Any departure from seeing the patient in an ordinary clinical setting should be part of a thoughtful treatment plan and documented as such.

Payment

Psychiatric treatment is hard work and requires disciplined effort and significant sacrifice. Those who have reached that level of expertise deserve to be paid for their activities. It is accepted in society that professionals offer specialized knowledge and skill in the service of others but that they also receive appropriate compensation for this work.

Psychiatric residents, in particular, are often somewhat reluctant to charge a fee for their appointments because they feel they are not deserving or not sufficiently trained to warrant payment. Part of professionalism, however, is accepting that a fiduciary relationship involves an occupation requiring a good deal of training and knowledge to impart a service. Even in a setting in which the patient does not directly pay the psychiatrist, the clinician is still in a paid profession. When a beginning psychiatrist or resident feels guilty about being compensated, the first step down the slippery slope may be to stop charging for the service. This decision insidiously alters the frame of the treatment in such a way that the patient may assume that special favors are required or that there needs to be some kind of reciprocity. Hence clarity about the charge for the session and the method of payment must be a high priority at the beginning of the work together.

Language and Clothing

Both language and clothing are often overlooked in discussions of professional boundaries. A professional talks in professional language to a patient. Obscenities, crude terms for sex, and sexually provocative language must be avoided. A degree of respect is required for a professional relationship, and coarse language can convey disrespect. Similarly, professional dress is essential to emphasize the professional role and the boundaries of the situation. Psychiatrists must try to anticipate how patients will react to what they wear and avoid excessively informal or revealing clothing when meeting with patients. In recent years, young physicians have visible tattoos, body piercing, distinctive hairstyles, jewelry, or dress that suggests certain lifestyles, roles, or commitments outside of their roles as physicians. A doctor's appearance does influence the therapeutic frame and can be experienced as creating either a sense of closeness and similarity or distance and dissimilarity between the clinician and patient. Just as a doctor's gender, age, and physical size may stimulate certain responses that have importance in shaping transference, these other factors affecting appearance and demeanor carry significance for patients as well. Some earlier-career psychiatrists have a difficult time anticipating how patients will react to what they wear—another example in which one's capacity to mentalize is crucial to professionalism. These clothing guidelines may be difficult to follow when someone is called into a hospital or a clinic on the weekend or in the evening when they are not dressed for work. One must take these possibilities into account when they are on call or expecting a possible crisis with a patient.

Self-Disclosure

Let us begin the discussion of self-disclosure with a clinical example.

> Dr. Phillips arrived at her appointment with Mr. Wilson about 10 minutes late. When Mr. Wilson came into the office, he said to Dr. Phillips, "It's not like you to be late. Is everything OK?"
>
> Dr. Phillips hesitated for a moment and then disclosed the following information: "Well, I might as well tell you that I was visiting my mother in the hospital. She's seriously ill, and I'm not sure if she's going to make it."
>
> Mr. Wilson thanked Dr. Phillips for her candor and said he appreciated knowing what was going on since he cared about her. Dr. Phillips felt relieved because she could not see that her disclosure did any kind of harm. Dr. Phillips then tried to shift the focus onto Mr. Wilson, but he asked about her mother's diagnosis. Dr. Phillips hesitated, then told him that the diagnosis was unclear and that they had a neurologist and neurosurgeon involved to try to figure out what was going on. Mr. Wilson asked if they thought it might be some kind of stroke or hemorrhage and said that his dad had had a hemorrhagic stroke that he had never recovered from. Dr. Phillips said that she did not really know and would keep him posted.

Dr. Phillips felt a little guilty and uncomfortable about having ventilated her own concerns, but the session went on and ended adequately.
However, for the next several sessions, Mr. Wilson began each hour with
questions about her mother. Dr. Phillips welcomed the opportunity to
discuss it since her patient was a sympathetic listener. Finally, however,
she realized that she was billing him for time in which she talked about
her own problems and her own family life. She told him that she thought
they should not discuss it anymore. Mr. Wilson said, "With whom can
you discuss it if you're not talking about it with me?"

Dr. Phillips suddenly realized that he was starting to perform a function for her that was not part of the professional role and reassured him
that she had others to talk to. Clearly, she had opened a door into her
private life with her self-disclosing, and Mr. Wilson had taken advantage
of the opening by asking more personal questions.

The case of Dr. Phillips reflects the perils that are inherent in disclosing
one's personal problems or family information to a patient. Although patients may be ready to listen and be helpful, it is not their obligation to take
care of their treating clinicians. Moreover, the initial self-disclosure led to
a whole series of disclosures about what was happening with Dr. Phillips's
mother in a way that was not useful in the long run for the therapy. Finally,
it misled the patient to think it was "open season" on his doctor's private
life.

It is impossible to be totally anonymous as a psychotherapist. One is
sending out information about one's beliefs, biases, background, and personality all the time in the interaction with the patient. In addition, patients
can access all kinds of information about the therapist through the Internet.
Nevertheless, patients "need" their doctors to be focused on therapeutic
goals, not "using" the doctor-patient relationship to give emotional sustenance or support to the clinician. Moreover, beyond the issue of inappropriate emotional relief or gratification of the caregiver, psychotherapists and
other clinicians need a zone of privacy to feel secure in their professional
role.

Self-disclosure does have therapeutic value in some circumstances. There
is no absolute "litmus test" for what is "good" or "bad" self-revelation, and
indeed, in practice, the dividing line between beneficial and non-beneficial
disclosure can be difficult. The clinician must be very purposeful and
thoughtful, asking oneself the question, "Does this comment help the patient?" Does the self-revelation help engage the patient, create a greater
sense of rapport, or provide reinforcement for a healthy impulse or behavior of the patient? In more concrete terms, one can draw a line at offering

information about one's family or about one's personal problems. Chitchat at the beginning of a session sometimes leads one to talk about movies, sporting events, or other activities that may reveal information in a limited way, but such information does not burden the patient in the way that more emotionally charged personal problems or family issues may. Some personal information, such as the psychiatrist's pets or the psychiatrist's favorite sports team, may not burden the patient either, and these kinds of disclosures may actually facilitate a therapeutic alliance with the patient, so some flexibility is needed.

Certain kinds of disclosures may be therapeutic in the sense of helping the patient mentalize about the psychotherapist's experience. For example, provocative patients may stir up feelings in the clinician that may be usefully shared. If, for example, a male patient is talking about his female psychiatrist in a way that is making her uncomfortable, it may be beneficial for him to know that his desire to turn the tables by making his therapist—rather than himself—uncomfortable is a misuse of the therapeutic session. Hence the therapist might say, "Mr. Ross, when you look at my legs and talk about them in that way, it concerns me. I feel like you're trying to transform the therapy into a situation in which you are in control and I am the one who is uncomfortable, as a way of dealing with your own discomfort." Some countertransference feelings should not be disclosed to the patient. Saying, "I hate that about you!" or "I have sexual feelings for you" may create serious problems in the therapeutic relationship and even cause the patient to quit coming to see the psychiatrist. Hence one needs to be judicious in using self-disclosure and to think carefully about the potential implication for the treatment.

There is another kind of self-disclosure that is based on self-absorption in the psychiatrist and a tendency to monopolize the conversation with irrelevant personal comments. In a study of physicians' self-disclosure in primary care visits, McDaniel et al. (2007), using unannounced, undetected, standardized patients, examined 113 recorded transcripts and found that in 34% of new visits with these patients, practicing primary care physicians disclosed information about themselves or their personal relationships. Some of these self-disclosures appeared to be quite disruptive, and there was no evidence of any positive effect. We would like to think that psychiatrists are more empathically attuned to their patients, but it is not uncommon for patients to seek out another treater because of having a psychiatrist who obliviously rambles on about himself or herself. One college student switched to a new psychiatrist because she became fed up with the way her previous psychiatrist talked about his own college experiences, his final exams, and his specific grades for each course during their therapy sessions.

Gifts

Many grateful patients wish to express their appreciation to a psychiatrist who has helped them. The psychiatric clinician must always consider these gifts on a case-by-case basis governed by several issues: the expense of the gift, the determination of whether it is in the patient's best interest to accept a gift, and the potential risk of devastating the patient by declining the gift. The ultimate decision involves clinical judgments that may be nuanced in nature, and sometimes the psychiatric resident simply is not sure what to do. In such situations, one always has the option of saying that it is necessary to check with one's supervisor before deciding if the gift can be accepted. One can graciously explain that there are policies in the clinic that have to be discussed and clarified. Most residents feel insecure in this area, and a survey of both medical students and residents found that they felt a need for additional training regarding how to interact with families and patients around gifts (Roberts et al. 2005b).

A case example illustrates the challenges in sorting out the ethical and therapeutic implications of gifts in treatment.

> A young female psychiatric resident had worked with a severely ill patient with multiple addictions and self-destructive behaviors. After a long period of establishing predictability and trust, the patient began to make considerable progress in his life, returning to school to become an emergency medical technician, stopping all illicit substance use, and engaging in less chaotic interactions with his family of origin.
>
> One year after the initiation of treatment, the patient returned "home" for Thanksgiving and shortly thereafter began to do poorly. He relapsed into some drug use and felt emotionally more "out of control," although his school attendance and behavior remained steady. He revealed that he was sexually abused by a male family member who was present at Thanksgiving, and dealing with the set of issues arising in their interactions during the family trip was the substance of the next few sessions with the psychiatrist. The patient's rage at having been "used" by the family member and the fact that his parents had not protected him sufficiently were the dominant themes expressed by the patient, who also expressed pride at not having completely "fallen off the wagon" after the Thanksgiving trip.

The day before Christmas, the patient arrived for his usual session with a poinsettia plant for the psychiatric resident, and later that day a gift of diamond earrings arrived, unbeknownst to the patient, for the psychiatrist from his parents. The psychiatrist immediately returned the earrings, a gift she felt to be problematic for many reasons, but in discussion with her supervisor ultimately decided to keep the poinsettia. She and the patient together decided to place it in the waiting area of the clinic. She introduced the issue of the gifts gently into the patient's treatment, which continued to progress well.

This illustration involving not one but two gifts is very revealing. The gift from the patient, a poinsettia, was symbolic, culturally congruent, and not costly. Its symbolism was discussed openly in the session with the psychiatrist and patient and the decision to place the poinsettia in the clinic's waiting room had an altruistic and generous "feel" to it, which was itself a positive experience for the patient. The expensive gift from the parents introduced more difficult and potentially damaging meanings into the treatment situation, and keeping the earrings—depending on how they were, in fact, motivated—would have sent a message of collusion, absolution, and/or self-interested gain back to the parents. The fact that they were sent without the patient's knowledge was also important to the therapeutic process and could have disrupted the alliance between the patient and the psychiatrist, were it handled differently.

The decision is easier when a psychiatrist is approached by a wealthy patient who wishes to make a large donation to the psychiatrist's clinic or research project. This represents a conflict of interest for the psychiatrist. Specifically, if psychiatrists start to think about a patient as a potential donor, their therapeutic purpose becomes clouded with concerns about facilitating the donation instead of helping the patient deal with difficult issues. They may become less confrontational and promote idealization in the transference. As Roberts et al. (2006) noted, psychiatrists have an ethical duty to place therapeutic issues above all other interests. The offer of gifts may be a way of diverting the clinician's attention from aggression or negative feelings. It may also be an unconscious "bribe" to influence the clinician to avoid shameful and embarrassing issues in the treatment (Gutheil and Gabbard 1993).

In academic psychiatry safeguards can be built into the department or medical school that assure the separation of philanthropy from clinical settings (Roberts et al. 2006). Psychiatrists who treat wealthy philanthropists tend to have blind spots regarding their potential to influence their patients to make gifts that might ultimately benefit them. Hence they must keep the treatment relationship uncontaminated by such considerations and focus only on the patient's treatment concerns. An advisory workgroup may be useful to consider potential donations in terms of their ethical implications. The chief goal is to maintain clear role separation, such that a treating clinician has no involvement whatsoever with a decision about a donation and does not receive any direct benefit from a gift.

Most psychiatrists who practice psychotherapy feel that it is acceptable to take a gift from a patient at the time of termination, provided it is reasonably inexpensive. Turning down such a gift may destroy the patient's alliance with the therapist, and because it would be the last session when the decline occurred, there would be no subsequent opportunity to discuss the impact on the patient.

Physical Contact

Physical contact is generally discouraged in the psychiatrist-patient relationship. A handshake is common, but rarely does physical contact go beyond that, except in extraordinary circumstances. One patient tripped coming into the doctor's office, and the therapist responded humanely and helped her to her feet. A patient who experiences a horrible loss and is sobbing may reach out to the therapist for a hug. In such situations, one might return the hug instead of rejecting the patient's plea for comfort.

The physician should not initiate a hug, however, even if she or he feels it might provide consolation or be helpful to the patient. One cannot know in advance how that hug would be experienced by the patient. The clinician's intent may not be the same as how the patient experiences the impact of the hug (Gabbard 2008). Even therapists who are proficient at mentalizing may misread the patient. Patients who are paranoid may feel severely violated. Patients with a history of childhood sexual abuse may feel sexually assaulted. Table 3–2 summarizes some guiding principles in considering physical contact.

As one of the guiding principles, the therapist is cautioned against touching a patient who has erotic transference. Although this is good advice, one must keep in mind that we often do not know if a patient has erotic feelings because such feelings are either unconscious or undisclosed. Similarly, one

---

TABLE 3–2.   Physical contact in psychiatric treatment

A handshake is usually a reasonable boundary of physical contact.

One may consider responding to a hug initiated under extraordinary circumstances or at the end of the last session of a long treatment. Even under such circumstances, a clinician should be concerned about any message that he or she may be conveying to the patient.

Clinicians should avoid initiating hugs.

Anytime there is clear erotic transference in the patient, physical contact should be avoided, because even light touches can be exciting to the patient.

If a hug or other physical contact occurs with a patient during the course of psychotherapy, the meaning of that contact should be explored and discussed rather than compartmentalized and avoided.

Repetitive hugging has no place in psychiatric treatment, even though it may be routine in other settings, such as a 12-step program.

---

may not be aware of a history of sexual abuse that makes a patient particularly sensitive to feeling violated. The bottom line is that when it comes to physical contact, there is no safe harbor where one can be free of concern. Therapists must be cautious and err on the conservative side when in doubt.

One of the strongest reasons to refrain from physical contact is that the slippery slope often creeps up on the practitioner in a way that is barely noticeable. A touch on the shoulder can later be transformed into a hug. A hug can later include a kiss, and sexual contact may ultimately emerge from rationalizations that the patient was deprived as a child and therefore needs physical affection as an adult to make up for that deficit in childhood. Some patients will make a plea to the psychotherapist and say such things as, "Your words do not help me. I need to be held because I was not loved as a child. It has nothing to do with sex. It's just a longing for love." As noted in Chapter 1, psychiatrists, like other clinicians, can be masters of self-deception and convince themselves that a departure from the usual boundaries will be beneficial in a particular case. The distinction between love and sex or between a nonsexual hug and an erotic hug is elusive in the therapeutic setting, and discretion is the better part of valor. Moreover, from the patient's perspective, there may be no difference whatsoever.

Boundary Crossings Versus Boundary Violations

No psychiatric practitioner is able to transcend countertransference enactments that may occur when patients strike a nerve in us that causes us to react in a way that later we may regret. Patients may talk about a loss that resonates with the therapist's loss, and the therapist may extend the hour beyond the usual 50 minutes. In the midst of a family crisis, therapists may disclose aspects of their own personal lives to a patient in a way that burdens the patient. These enactments may subsequently be discussed with the patient productively and may even help the therapeutic process if the patient can learn something from them. Part of what patients learn in such situations is that the therapist is human.

These minor transgressions are frequently referred to as *boundary crossings* rather than *boundary violations* (Gabbard 2008; Gabbard and Lester 2003; Gutheil and Gabbard 1993). Boundary crossings usually occur as unusual events in the therapy that are discussable and create no permanent damage to the therapy or the patient. They are not always countertransference enactments. Sometimes they are conscious departures from the usual frame in extraordinary situations, such as returning the hug of a patient who has suffered a devastating loss or deliberating extending a session until a patient has been able to stop sobbing and leave the office in a more composed state of mind.

Boundary violations, on the other hand, tend to be repetitive, egregious, and create irreparable damage to the therapeutic process and to the patient. Often the therapist insists they do not need to be discussed because they are part of the "real relationship." It is almost always a "red flag" in psychotherapy if something that happens in the therapy is not discussable between the therapist and patient. Boundary violations often occur in a progressive descent down a slippery slope of ever-increasing transgressions. They may involve frank sexual contact between therapist and patient, but they also may stop short of that and still cause serious problems in therapy. In essence, boundary violations are transgressions that undermine the positive therapeutic commitments of the therapeutic relationship.

Table 3–3 illustrates the distinction between crossings and violations.

TABLE 3–3. **Boundary crossings versus boundary violations**

Boundary crossings	Boundary violations
Benign and even helpful breaks in the frame	Exploitative breaks in the frame
Usually occur in isolation	Usually repetitive
Minor and attenuated in most cases	Egregious and often extreme (e.g., sexual misconduct)
Therapist and patient may discuss in therapy	Therapist generally discourages discussion in therapy
Ultimately do not cause harm to patient	Typically cause harm to the patient and/or the therapy

Source. Gabbard GO: *Long-Term Psychodynamic Psychotherapy: A Basic Text,* 2nd Edition. Washington, DC, American Psychiatric Publishing, 2010

Posttermination Sexual Contacts

Professional Boundaries After Termination

A core component of professionalism is maintaining a professional relationship with the patient. Professionalism should not connote rigidity or a looseness. On the contrary, it means establishing an interpersonal warmth and caring that allow the patient to open up and feel understood. Too great a concern about boundary violations can lead to an inflexible position on the part of the psychiatrist that drives the patient away. On the other hand, clinicians can think they are helping a patient by responding emotionally, when actually they are meeting their own needs and ruining the patient's chance of receiving help. One must always remember that feelings of love for the patient do not justify departures from the professional role and physical or sexual relations with the patient. Ethics codes proscribe certain behaviors that are potentially damaging to the patient *regardless of the feelings or intent* behind those behaviors. Love or compassion are not mitigating factors that justify boundary violations.

For psychiatrists, the notion of a sexual relationship after termination has clear consequences. Sex with a patient after termination is just as unethical as sex with a patient during treatment. The American Psychiatric Association determined in 1993 that all sexual relationships between a psychiatrist and a former patient are unethical (American Psychiatric Association 2001) whether psychotherapy was involved or not and no matter how much time has expired since termination. For other physicians there is a little more flexibility on post-termination relationships—each case must be considered on its own merits. Once again, psychiatrists are held to a higher standard. The reasons for the absolute prohibition are clear. Transference and the power differential inherent in the doctor-patient relationship continue. All studies of posttermination follow-up involving psychotherapy and psychoanalytic patients demonstrate that transference is instantly reestablished (Gabbard 2002).

Another compelling reason to have an absolute prohibition against posttermination sexual relationships is that the consequences of making such sexual contact acceptable would have a devastating impact on psychotherapy. If it were in the mind of both patient and therapist that a romantic relationship were possible someday, it might well alter the way the two interact. The patient might conceal any shameful sexual episodes from the past to make sure that he or she remained appealing to the therapist, and the therapist might avoid confrontation about areas of the patient's life that would make the patient angry. In other words, a mutually idealizing relationship could be fostered that would undermine effective psychotherapy. The final reason for the absolute ban on post-termination sexual relationships is that patients often return. One never knows if a termination is final or not.

Because of the uncertainty about the need for further treatment, nonsexual boundaries should also be monitored after termination (Gabbard and Lester 2003). Obviously, the psychiatrist who treats colleagues or other professionals may have contact after termination. Similarly, individuals who live in small communities and have overlapping roles (e.g., as neighbors, school board members) will naturally cross paths again and perhaps often. The psychiatrist can certainly interact in a friendly way and make it clear that he or she is glad to see the former patient. However, it will be important to not convey to others their preexisting relationship and is generally a good idea not to share personal problems with the patient or become intimate friends, because that may remove the opportunity for the patient to return for more treatment. Keeping in mind the potential for return is a good way to moderate the degree of closeness in post-termination relationships.

Prevention

The first word on prevention is that psychotherapy involves a radical form of privacy that cannot be monitored without breaching confidentiality. Therefore, we will never be able to completely eradicate all sexual boundary violations (Gabbard and Lester 2003). Nevertheless, psychiatric residents should have systematic training on issues related to exploitation of patients and the impulse toward personal gratification that may arise in psychiatrists as they conduct their work. In addition, it is important to emphasize good habits around professional boundaries and the prevention of boundary violations (Vamos 2001). However, under the influence of strong feelings toward the patient, one may dismiss all the education one has had on the subject and make a self-deceiving case for being an exception so that one does not have to relinquish the powerful feelings of love or desire for the patient. Hence education is no panacea.

Probably the best preventive of all is to arrange for ongoing consultation throughout one's career. Introducing a consultant into the doctor-patient relationship makes it less secretive and more accessible to outside influence. The psychiatrist who has a consultant often feels as though the consultant enters the room as an internal presence in the session with the patient. Clinical psychiatrists, especially those who intend to do psychotherapy, should seek out a senior consultant with whom they can share their countertransference feelings openly and comfortably—someone they trust who will also tell them, before it is too late, when they are entering a minefield.

Both consultation and supervision can be undermined, of course, by the failure to honestly report what is going on in the treatment. Psychiatric residents should get into the practice of making a concerted effort to share with their supervisor the things they are most ashamed of in their learning of psychotherapy. In fact, supervisors can facilitate this candor by telling their supervisees that the aspects of therapy that they most want to conceal from the supervisor are the very things that should be brought up so they can obtain assistance in thinking through therapeutic strategies. The fear of getting a critical evaluation from the supervisor may keep the supervisee from learning.

A variation of this theme, when one is out of supervision and in practice, is to think about a consultant in a similar manner. In other words, one of the best forms of self-monitoring is to ask oneself, "Is there anything I'm doing in the treatment that I could not share with a consultant?" If the answer is "yes," then a consultation is urgently needed (Gabbard 2008).

Conclusion

As the title of this chapter suggests, much of professionalism in the clinical relationship goes beyond simply adhering to professional boundaries. Much of effective communication and interaction in the doctor-patient relationship has to do with a sincere effort by doctors to place themselves in the minds of their patients. In psychiatry we place a good deal of emphasis on mentalizing when working with seriously disturbed patients (Allen et al. 2008), where the therapist recognizes the mind of the patient and tries to help the patient come to know the minds of others as a way of understanding the subjectivity of perceptions. In other words, patients come to learn that they are not perceiving things in a way that reflects absolute truth. Rather, their perceptions are based on a subjective perspective based on their own life experiences, and other people will perceive such situations differently based on their background. Hence a good psychiatrist is trying to appreciate that the patient's perspective is different. As we described earlier in the chapter, hugs often misfire because a psychiatrist does not recognize that what is meant as a caring gesture can be perceived by someone else's mind as an assault. Psychiatrists need to ask themselves a question, "How am I coming across to this patient based on this patient's unique features?"

Beyond mentalizing, there is a practical aspect to the doctor-patient relationship, what Kahn (2008) referred to as "etiquette-based medicine." This approach emphasizes good manners, a concept that has perhaps lost its central place in American society in recent years. Kahn stressed that such etiquette involves a mental checklist about things to do when one is with a patient. For example, he suggested that when a physician enters a hospital room, he or she should shake hands, smile, explain his or her role, and ask the patient how he or she feels. Kahn emphasized that even those who do not innately have the capacity for expert mentalizing or empathy can still learn the principles of how to behave when with a patient. He noted that it is far easier to change behavior than attitudes. Good behavior is just as important as compassion for the patient.

Key Points

- Professional boundaries create an optimal environment for the psychiatrist to behave in a professional role that is designed to be helpful in diagnosing and treating the patient's problems. What a psychiatrist says and does are all for the overarching purpose of helping the patient with the problems the patient brings to the clinical setting.

- Confidentiality in psychiatry is of paramount importance as a component of professionalism, and it includes not revealing whether one is treating a patient, not sharing what one learns in a clinical setting with anyone but a supervisor or consultant, and not acting outside the therapeutic relationship on information that one receives from a patient.

- The time and place of a clinical contact with a patient ordinarily involve scheduled meetings in a hospital, clinic, or private office setting. Clinical appointments can take place outside those usual settings, but they should be part of a carefully thought-out treatment plan and documented in the patient's record.

- Self-disclosure is bound to happen in one form or another, and it is unreasonable to try to avoid all forms of self-disclosure. In general, one should avoid comments about one's personal problems or family. Comments that might burden the patient in some way should also be avoided. Self-disclosures may be helpful to patients at times when they involve here-and-now interactions that may help the patient understand what he or she does to create reactions in others.

- The decision to accept or decline a gift from a patient must be made on a case-by-case basis according to what is in the patient's best interest, the value of the gift, and the meaning of the gift within the clinical relationship.

- Any sexual contact between a psychiatrist and a patient is considered unethical during the clinical relationship as well as after it ends.

- Nonsexual boundaries following termination of the clinical relationship are less well defined, but a good practice is to keep in mind that the patient may return for further consultation or treatment.

- One of the most effective measures to prevent boundary violations is consultation or supervision with a senior clinician on difficult clinical situations throughout one's career.

Chapter 4

Professionalism and Boundaries in Cyberspace

As noted in Chapter 3, *boundaries* have traditionally been defined as the elements of the therapeutic frame—that is, location, time of appointment, absence of physical contact, avoidance of self-disclosure, and confidentiality. In the past two decades, however, the expanded dimensions of the Internet have altered the landscape of boundaries and even professionalism. Patients today expect to use electronic communication for most professional service interactions (Seeman et al. 2010). Some mental health practitioners are even offering e-therapy now. In addition, the capacity to search for all forms of information through search engines, such as Google, has expanded phenomenally in the past decade and eroded traditional therapist anonymity. Moreover, social networking sites such as Facebook have allowed the sharing of personal information among millions of people throughout the world. Personal and professional details are now available in a way that is redefining privacy for everyone and redefining boundaries and professionalism for psychiatrists and other mental health practitioners.

The practice of medicine and psychiatry has historically preceded the development of ethics codes and laws to regulate new developments in practice

(Kassaw and Gabbard 2002). To a large extent the professional boundaries associated with cyberspace are evolving as we write these words. We need to educate psychiatrists and other mental health professionals about the ethics and professionalism concerns deriving from practices in cyberspace and continue to be familiar with new technology as it develops. Gabbard et al. (2011) recently reviewed the professionalism issues, clinical dilemmas, and potential boundary problems related to these shifts in the accessibility to information today. The guidelines we provide in this chapter may be helpful in conceptualizing the risks involved with cybercommunication and preventing harm to patients and to practitioners.

E-mail

Because the vast majority of the public has the expectation that e-mail is acceptable for communication in personal service situations, psychiatrists and other mental health professionals cannot ignore the dilemma of how to respond to e-mail even if they wish to strictly limit their involvement on the Internet with their patients. Although there is hardly any case law regarding the doctor-patient relationship and e-mail, personally identifiable health information is protected under the Health Insurance Portability and Accountability Act (HIPAA) of 1996. This act requires certain measures to protect the security and privacy of health information, and some states have adopted additional safeguards for mental health records, such as password protection (Recupero 2005). The American Medical Association has developed some e-mail guidelines in which they suggest that there is no absolute prohibition against using unencrypted e-mail with patients, but they recommend encryption unless patients waive the option (American Medical Association 2005).

In discussing the ethics and boundary issues connected with e-mail, it is useful to distinguish between e-therapy and e-mail (Kassaw and Gabbard 2002; Recupero 2005). E-therapy carries a much greater risk than the simple use of e-mail to change an appointment or inform the doctor about a need for a prescription refill. E-therapy for all practical purposes is practicing medicine online. Kassaw and Gabbard (2002) pointed out that e-mail communication hinders first-rate psychiatric care because it lacks the central features of a therapeutic relationship. The clinician does not have data relevant to the mental status examination, such as affect, speech patterns, and other behavioral observations. Much of the assessment of suicide risk, for example, depends on nonverbal information observable in a face-to-face interview in an office. Moreover, in an urgent situation, the patient cannot know how soon the therapist will be reading e-mail. An overarching ethical concern is the misconception that e-mail is private. The very nature of e-mail can provide a false sense of security to both sender and reader. Most people have difficulty accepting the well-established premise that e-mail is roughly as private as a postcard. E-mail communications sit on a screen while read, and anyone who passes within a reasonable distance has the ability to read the content. Breaches of privacy relate directly to the vigilance of the sender. Virtually everyone knows stories about how an e-mail was sent to the wrong person. There may be HIPAA violations around every corner when one is communicating with patients via e-mail. All one has to do is hit the wrong key, and a name will automatically be typed in the "To" window that the therapist did not intend. The same problem, of course, can occur with the patient.

Another frequent problem encountered by psychiatrists, mental health professionals, and physicians is unsolicited e-mail. Patients commonly use search engines to locate medical information online. It is often with the best of intentions that practitioners respond to these unsolicited e-mails by trying to provide helpful information. However, if information is provided, and the patient follows the psychiatrist's advice, this interaction may establish a doctor-patient relationship from a legal standpoint (Recupero 2005). One could also be vulnerable to a lawsuit because an argument could be made that it is difficult for a psychiatrist to provide competent medical or psychiatric evaluation or treatment without a face-to-face initial evaluation.

Because of the widespread use of e-mail for multiple situations in everyday life, many practitioners are feeling increasingly comfortable with simple e-mails that involve the rescheduling of an appointment or clarifying the correct dosage of a medication, or arranging for a physician to call in a refill. However, often these types of concerns blend into more complex clinical situations.

Dr. Atkins had been treating Mrs. Schiller in combined pharmacotherapy and psychotherapy for about 4 months. One evening at home he was reading his e-mail, and he received a message from Mrs. Schiller that said, "I wanted to ask you about the Lexapro. I think it's helping me feel calmer, but I'm not sure that I really feel like myself. I feel sort of numbed and detached from my day-to-day experiences and find that I really don't feel like crying at things that would ordinarily make me cry. Do we cut back on the dose by 5 mg to see if that might take this side effect away?" Dr. Atkins mulled over the e-mail and found himself wanting to dispense with it quickly as he did with other e-mails. Yet he realized that questions about the goal of the medication as well as the patient's sense of self were imbedded in her e-mail, and these questions needed to be addressed in person. Hence he wrote back, "Thank you for your e-mail, Mrs. Schiller. I'd like you to call for an appointment tomorrow morning so we can discuss these matters in person. I feel they are too complex for e-mail discussion. I look forward to speaking with you soon."

In this clinical vignette, Dr. Atkins is making decisions in his evolving experience with e-mail communication regarding which situations can genuinely be dealt with by hitting the "reply" button and which require face-to-face discussion. All practitioners must develop some guidelines of this nature. A good many professional organizations are now recommending that a practitioner obtain informed consent prior to initiating e-mail communication with existing patients (Recupero 2005). Patients need to understand the risks to confidentiality, the risk that their practitioner may not read e-mail as frequently as they imagine, and the inadvisability of using e-mail in a clinical emergency such as suicide.

Guidelines for E-mail Use

Although the American Medical Association has listed guidelines regarding the use of e-mail by physicians (Lewers 2000), they do not consider most mental health issues appropriate for e-mail communication. Obviously, privacy issues may be more damaging to mental health patients, and psychiatric practice varies widely from medication management to psychoanalysis to public hospital treatment. A "one-size-fits-all" policy on e-mail communication is probably not practical. Nevertheless, several recommendations may be considered and used according to one's practice setting. These recommendations are drawn from thoughtful articles by Seeman et al. (2010), Recupero (2005), and Kassaw and Gabbard (2002).

1. The psychiatrist or other mental health professional should not initiate a discussion of e-mail, because it may imply to the patient that some aspect of the treatment is trivial or not appropriate for face-to-

face discussion. The patient should be the one who brings up the issue and seeks guidelines for e-mail use.

2. The psychiatrist must define with the patient what is mutually acceptable for communication by e-mail. Hence psychiatrists may set limits in this regard and differ from the patient regarding what is reasonable for online correspondence.

3. Informed consent should be seriously considered, and this consent should involve a thorough discussion about who has access to the physician's e-mail and the various security risks on each end regarding unencrypted e-mail sent over the Internet. Patients must be informed that e-mails will be copied and placed within the medical record. During the discussion of informed consent, the clinician can also clarify that crises such as suicidality are not appropriate for e-mail. The clinician can also clarify that at all times he or she may insist on telephone or face-to-face contact in lieu of e-mail communication when a concern arises.

4. When a draft e-mail is being written, it is advisable to write the e-mail, proof and sign it before addressing it as one does a letter to ensure that it is not sent to the wrong person.

5. Encryption software should be carefully considered because it may offer the highest security possible. There are also Web-based services, such as e-Courier.ca, that offer high security without the installation of encryption software.

6. Clinicians must also be prepared to modify the understanding with the patient if excessive e-mails become a problem or if the content of the e-mails departs from the original conditions to which both parties agreed.

7. Clinicians should always inform the patient of reasonable amounts of time that may elapse before a reply to an e-mail is possible. They should be instructed to use the telephone to communicate an emergency situation.

8. In situations in which one receives unsolicited e-mail, clinicians must take care to ensure that a doctor-patient relationship is not accidentally created—the unknown e-mailer can be steered to a local physician or other mental health professional.

9. When one receives detailed clinical material in an e-mail from a current patient, the e-mail can be printed and discussed as part of the ongoing treatment (Gabbard 2001).

Obviously, these suggestions are only guidelines. Some dyads of patient and therapist may find uses that do not fall within these guidelines, like "checking in" when having a crisis or sending some good news to the therapist. Whatever is negotiated, however, should be carefully discussed in terms of potential difficulties.

Privacy and Anonymity in the Era of Cyberspace

For practitioners of psychoanalysis and psychotherapy, there is a long tradition of emphasizing asymmetry of disclosure within the therapeutic dyad. To some degree this set-up, which provides an ethical framework in which the emphasis is on the patient's issues rather than the therapist's concerns, entails some degree of comfort for the therapist. The rise of social networking and search engines has radically changed an asymmetrical frame of the doctor-patient relationship to the point where many would claim that we now practice in a "post-privacy era." Many mental health professionals are contacted by patients who first search the Internet for someone who might be a good fit according to areas of expertise, location, and even religious affiliation. In the course of using a search engine such as Google or Yahoo, one may also discover a good deal of information about the clinician's spouse or partner, children, and parents. In addition, they may read about the comments of other patients who had seen this clinician on one of a number of sites that post patient ratings of doctors. Some of the postings on these sites may be highly laudatory, even idealized, whereas others may be nasty and scathing and present a misleading picture of the doctor.

Dr. Marin was a 42-year-old psychiatrist who had seen a 24-year-old patient who was clearly addicted to opiates and was drug seeking. She had clarified that she was unable to prescribe the Tylenol #3 that he requested and gave him a good deal of information about outpatient and residential rehabilitation centers where he might work to withdraw from his opiate use and maintain abstinence. The patient was enraged and stomped out of her office. She later received an e-mail from a colleague who told her that she should read what was posted on one of the doctor-rating websites. She was horrified when she read the following post: "I had a terrible experience with Dr. Marin. I wouldn't refer my dog to her. She was callous, insensitive, and in a real hurry to get me out of her office. I had tried to establish a doctor-patient relationship with a new doctor in the city, and all I needed was the continuation of longstanding medication that has helped me with my chronic pain condition. She declared me an addict without taking a careful history, and she abruptly threw me out of her office without providing any alternative or even a temporary prescription to get me through until I found a new doctor. Avoid her like the plague!"

Fortunately for Dr. Marin, her colleague, who read the information, was the only one who brought it to her attention, and she was not aware of any adverse consequences from it. However, the example shows how reputations can be damaged without much recourse for the practitioner.

Public documents are accessible through search engines as well. Death certificates, marriage certificates, property tax documents, and various forms of genealogy are readily available for curious patients. Clinicians who have been trained in the traditional asymmetry of the treatment dyad are likely to feel exposed, invaded, and violated (Gabbard et al. 2011). Nevertheless, little can be done about the patient's freedom to search the Internet. The information available through Google or Yahoo searches is public. Moreover, the ethical principle of respect for the patient's autonomy prohibits the clinician from ordering a patient not to access information about the clinician's private life on the Internet. Indeed, such a prohibition would probably produce the opposite effect in that it would lead to unbearable curiosity about what the clinician wished to hide! Patients have no ethics code and therefore cannot "violate" professional boundaries in the same sense of an ethical breach when referring to clinicians and boundary violations. They can, of course, push the boundaries or test the limits, as is discussed in Chapter 5. However, when patients access public information about therapists, clinicians have little recourse except to explore the impact of the information on the patient and the process. They may also contact Web site administrators when erroneous information is accessible.

Finally, some trainees and clinicians might not appreciate that the Internet is also a permanent record of one's activities that cannot simply be erased at a later point in one's career. *The New York Times* recently reported on the impact of Web material on careers (Rosen 2010). A 66-year-old therapist from Canada was denied permission to cross the border into the United States because a border guard's Internet search revealed that he had written an article in a philosophy journal describing his experiments with drug use 30 years earlier. Although it was once said that the Internet offered the opportunity of reinventing ourselves, it now seems apparent that the Internet is shackling us to everything we ever said or ever did.

When Doctors
Google Patients

One could argue that "turnabout is fair play," and if the patient can Google the doctor, why can't the doctor Google the patient? The issue is more complicated than that simple aphorism suggests. Clinton et al. (2010) raise some serious concerns about the practice of a therapist "checking up" on his or her patient through a search. They suggest that there is a potential breach of the patient's trust when one secretly decides to Google the patient. Obviously, the context may be different depending on the psychiatric setting. A forensic evaluator, for example, tries to access maximal collateral information to provide a complete and comprehensive evaluation. Hence information in the public domain is not a violation of a sacred trust in the forensic setting as it might be in psychotherapy.

In the psychotherapeutic relationship, patients may bring up a blog, a Web site, or other information about themselves. Some even leap out of their chair and head toward the therapist's computer to show something on line to the therapist. This movement toward a private computer desk in the therapist's office may create some concern. What if there is a chart of another patient lying on the computer table? What if there are names of other patients or personal information on the computer screen itself? Should clinician and patient spend time together on the computer in any circumstance whatsoever? Is it more likely a flight from important therapeutic material that should be discussed face to face? These questions cannot be answered generically and may vary with the age of the patient and the type of therapy. In any case, boundary considerations must be taken into account.

The ethics issue inherent in seeking out information on one's patients is controversial. Not everyone agrees that this information should be off limits. Some would suggest that any information may be useful in the therapy. Many therapists would agree, however, that if this sort of information is pursued, one must be mindful of maintaining a good therapeutic alliance. Toward that end, some would argue that the search for the material should take place in the *presence* of the patient rather than "behind the patient's back" after he or she leaves the office. Moreover, what would it say about a therapist's countertransference if leisure time were being spent pursuing cyberdata on a patient?

By their very nature, clinicians who choose psychotherapy as a career are curious people who have a touch of voyeuristic interest in knowing details about others. They may find that they are going down a slippery slope when they begin to spend time in the session with their patient looking at various items that may relate to the patient. Once they begin this trend, what if the patient wants them to read other material, and they decline because they do not feel it is the best use of the time? What if the patient in that situation asks the therapist to read it between sessions? What if a patient begins to expect the therapist to read her blog on a regular basis?

Clinton et al. (2010) suggested that clinicians who are contemplating a search about their patient should be doing a good deal of self-reflection on their reasons for the search, how it might adversely affect the therapy, and how much of the results should be shared with the patient. Therapists may also need to prepare themselves for questions from patients about their policy regarding searches about their patients. A more fundamental ethical question is raised by this whole area of discourse: Does not a patient have the right to keep aspects of him- or herself private from the therapist in light of our general principle that psychotherapy should not be coercive?

Social Networking Sites and Blogs

Social networking sites such as MySpace and Facebook have profoundly altered the nature of privacy as a social norm. Facebook began as a network for college students, but it has since grown into an international social network site of more than 550,000,000 members. On Facebook, members routinely bare their souls about the most gut-wrenching phenomena as well as the most quotidian daily trivia that reflect the fabric of their lives. Sexual proclivities, intimate details of sexual encounters, and the wildest of fantasies are all routinely shared on Facebook and often greeted with a yawn by the millions of readers. As one journalist noted, "Dwindling secrets and prying eyes are at the heart of the Facebook conundrum. While offering an efficient and far-reaching way for people to bond, this site has also eroded natural barriers" (Stone 2009). To a large extent, users of Facebook under age 30 are using e-mail less often as they increasingly prefer to communicate almost entirely through Facebook.

A medical intern wrote an account in the *New England Journal of Medicine* in which he described how a patient had asked to add him as a friend on Facebook (Jain 2009). After some careful consideration of the implication of having someone in the dual relationship of "Facebook friend" and patient, he declined the offer. As a friend, that person has complete access to the doctor's profile on Facebook that includes pictures, personal information, and family data. The material placed on Facebook by a clinician is generally far more revealing than what is disclosed in the treatment relationship (Gabbard et al. 2011). Photographs can be "tagged" in such a way that they appear on other Facebook users' sites without the knowledge or consent of the person in the photograph. Although privacy settings are an option on Facebook, many do not bother with them. Hence the content of the profile is often available to users who are not even accepted "friends." One study (Thompson et al. 2008) found that only 37.5% of medical students and residents used their privacy settings. In the same study, some of the residents' and medical students' profiles revealed photographs in which alcohol was being used and other unprofessional content such as overt sexuality, foul language, and use of other substances.

This common use of Facebook as a forum for personal expression has served to underscore the fact that professionalism is not limited to work hours or work settings for physicians, psychiatrists, and other mental health professionals. If one has chosen a career in psychiatry, one must be prepared for the expectation that in any public setting, including those in cyberspace, one must exercise professionalism. What one does in the privacy of one's home is no one else's business. However, increasingly there are instances where Facebook photos have had deleterious effects on professional pursuits. Some applicants for postresidency positions, for example, have discovered that interviewers who may have influence over potential employment have surveyed information about them on Facebook.

A teacher in training posted a photo of herself at a party on her MySpace page (Rosen 2010). She was drinking from a cup with the caption "Drunken Pirate." The photo was deemed "unprofessional" by her supervisor, and her university denied her a teaching degree. In an ensuing lawsuit claiming that the university had violated her First Amendment rights by punishing her for after-hours behavior, a federal district judge in 2008 was not sympathetic to that point of view. He found that because the teacher in training was a public employee whose photo was not related to public concerns, her controversial photo on MySpace was not protected speech (Rosen 2010).

Another concern about information posted on Facebook is that in some cases, patients are mentioned casually in a way that individuals could be identified. This type of confidentiality breach is clearly unethical, and those who talk about their work must be sensitive to revealing anything that might suggest a patient's identity. Guidelines regarding disguise and patient consent for publication (Gabbard 2000) are rarely followed in these postings. Similarly, clinicians must be wary about commenting about groups of patients in a way that may appear to be pejorative.

Blogging can be even more problematic for psychiatrists and other mental health professionals. One has privacy settings on Facebook, but bloggers tend to share their ideas widely on Web links with others (Gabbard et al. 2011). A blog also leaves a record of past statements, whereas it is rather difficult to see what has been written in the past on a Facebook profile. Moreover, one blogger can copy material from another blogger and attribute it to the original author, so one never knows where it may end up.

Boundaries, Professionalism, and Clinical Dilemmas

As noted at the beginning of the chapter, the excursions into cyberspace by clinicians and patients have led to new ethical and clinical dilemmas for practitioners. Beauchamp (2009) outlined four clusters of moral principles that underlie the ethics codes relevant to medical practice: justice (i.e., fairness and how benefits and burdens are distributed); nonmaleficence (the fundamental principle of avoiding the potential for harm); respect for autonomy (acknowledgement that patients are free to make their own decisions); and beneficence (the equation of weighing risks vs. benefits). The situations that arise in cyberspace are varied, and some violate ethics whereas others clearly do not (Gabbard et al. 2011).

If one writes about patients on a blog or a social network site, there is clearly a potential to do harm through breach of confidentiality. Even if names are not mentioned, the patient may be identifiable, so this is clearly an ethics breach. If one attempts to engage in a dual relationship with a person who is both a "Facebook friend" and a psychiatric patient, a boundary

violation is established because of a violation of the principle of nonmaleficence. The reason that dual relationships are not acceptable is that the treatment setting is more effective if the psychiatrist will never be anything but
a treater, as noted in Chapter 3. Becoming a "friend" has the potential for
harm because it may raise false hope that the clinician is more than a professional doing a job.

Another ethical principle, respect for autonomy, is violated if the clinician tries to stop patients from accessing information about him or her on
the Internet. That principle makes it clear that psychiatrists should not be
in the position of placing constraints on the patient's freedom to pursue
public information. The discomfort that the therapist feels can be dealt
with through supervision, consultation, or personal treatment while helping the patient think about the meanings of his or her curiosity (Gabbard
et al. 2011).

Some of the concerns raised fall more in the category of professionalism than true boundary violations. As previously suggested, photos of a
professional drinking or using marijuana may represent a professionalism
problem simply by virtue of its accessibility. Patients who see such photos
may experience a loss of trust in the therapist they are seeing even though
the actual activity occurred outside duty hours. If one talks about groups
of patients in a pejorative way, no ethics code may have been violated, but
it is certainly unprofessional to be speaking of people with mental illness
in a disparaging way.

Still other issues do not fall in the category of professionalism or boundary disturbances. They are simply chance encounters that occur as a result
of the fact that cyberspace is a surprisingly small world.

> Dr. Billings was a 41-year-old divorced psychiatrist who accessed a dating
> Website to try to find a suitable partner. Much to his chagrin, his patient,
> Ms. Quinn, a 29-year-old single woman, saw him on the dating site be-
> cause she too was looking for a partner. She began one session by saying,
> "I see you're available." Dr. Billings was taken aback and responded with a
> simple, "What do you mean?" Ms. Quinn clarified: "Well, you and I are
> on the same dating site, and I saw your profile. I wondered if you'd been
> divorced since you don't wear a ring. I guess I had always assumed that you
> had a girlfriend, and it was kind of exciting to think of you as someone
> who is looking." Ms. Quinn smiled as she teased Dr. Billings about his
> availability. Dr. Billings felt exposed and embarrassed, and he quickly clar-
> ified that dating was not possible because of their professional relationship.
> Ms. Quinn seemed hurt at that admonition and shut down to the point
> where she was silent for a good 5 minutes. Dr. Billings recognized that he

had been rather abrupt and apologized, hoping to repair the rupture in the therapeutic alliance.

To his credit, Dr. Billings recognized that he had made a clumsy clinical error by shutting down the issue and shaming the patient. However, he realized that no boundary had been breached because he had not deliberately made an outside contact with Ms. Quinn. Rather, this type of incident falls in the category of an *extratherapeutic contact*. Such contacts occur all the time in life outside of therapy when one encounters a patient at a restaurant, a concert, or a professional meeting. One simply uses tact to avoid an embarrassing interaction when possible, or simply nods and smiles at the patient. In essence, the situation is the same in cyberspace, although it may come as more of a surprise, especially when romantic interests become the topic.

Information available from a Google search may similarly be uncomfortable, but the therapist must accept it as public information and therefore deal with it as a clinical matter. Patients sometimes use Google to get a bird's eye view of their therapist's home. They may also look up data on the cost of the house the therapist purchased. These matters must be dealt with clinically as well, even if there is a deliberate search rather than a chance encounter. In any case, a professionalism or ethics problem is not an accurate description of what has transpired.

Recommendations

Just as recommendations about e-mail must remain tentative and preliminary, suggestions about how to manage the other areas of cyberspace from a standpoint of professionalism and boundaries have to be conceptualized as a beginning effort to create safe zones and avoid problem areas within this new realm of interaction. Psychiatry as a specialty, of course, requires special attention because of the focus on the nuances of the doctor-patient relationship. Gabbard et al. (2011) developed a set of recommendations that are designed to prevent potential for harm in treatment and boundary violations in the professional relationship. These suggestions are also designed to maintain the type of professionalism to which all psychiatrists aspire. Because of the evolving nature of this area, they should be considered guidelines only:

1. Mental health professionals and psychiatrists who are on social networking sites should avail themselves of all possible privacy settings (Chretien et al. 2009; Guseh et al. 2009).
2. Psychiatrists and other mental health professionals who choose to search for information about one's patient must be prepared for clinical complications that require sensitive management. In light of the fact that some patients may experience such a search as a violation of their trust (White 2009), clinicians should consider the possibility of informing the patient and gaining the patient's consent for such an Internet exploration.
3. Several items should not be included on social networking sites or blogs. These include

   • Photographs that may be perceived as unprofessional (e.g., drinking, drug use, or sexually provocative poses)
   • Patient information or other confidential material
   • Any comment on administrative actions, lawsuits, or clinical cases in which one is currently involved, because there is a potential to compromise one's defense (PRMS 2009)
   • Disparaging comments about colleagues or groups of patients

4. Web searches should be conducted on a periodic basis to monitor false information or photographs of concern. If these items are discovered, the Web site administrator can be contacted with a request to remove problematic information.
5. All training institutions should develop policies for handling breaches of ethics or professionalism on the Internet.
6. Training institutions should educate their trainees about professionalism and boundary issues as part of their professionalism curriculum and assist them in the mastery of technology.
7. One should avoid becoming "Facebook friends" or entering into other dual relationships via the Internet with patients (Lagu et al. 2008; Stone 2009).
8. One must not assume that anything one posts with the intent of being anonymous will remain anonymous, because posts can be traced to their sources (PRMS 2009).
9. Psychiatric residents or other mental health professionals who want to be available on dating sites must be fully prepared to deal with reactions of patients who may see them.

10. Psychotherapy training should include consideration of the clinical dilemmas presented by blogging, search engines, social networking sites, and the potential boundary issues that arise from them.

Key Points

- The cyberrevolution has presented new issues of professionalism and boundaries for psychiatrists to manage.

- Few formal guidelines have been developed, and much is left to negotiations between psychiatrist and patient.

- If e-mail is used, clear guidelines for its use should be worked out with patients within a context of informed consent.

- Psychiatrists should familiarize themselves with phenomena such as social networking, blogging, and Googling.

- Privacy and anonymity of the clinician have been radically redefined, and therapists must accept that they cannot control what patients read about them on the Internet. It is public information, and the best they can do is to process the patient's reaction to reading the information.

- One should avoid becoming a "Facebook friend" with a patient, and those clinicians who use Facebook should be sure that privacy settings are in place.

- Photos and information about patients should not be placed on Facebook or blogs.

- Care should be used in Googling information about patients in light of the risk of having them feel violated by the therapist's intrusiveness.

Chapter 5

Professionalism Commitments

Inherent in the notion of professionalism is that the patient's needs are put ahead of the doctor's needs. Indeed, an altruistic commitment to help others who are suffering, even when it may be inconvenient for the physician, is part of a values system fundamental to medicine and psychiatry. However, as we noted in Chapter 1, self-interest cannot be eradicated, and balancing and managing self-interest must be a form of commitment that psychiatrists make when they set out on a career to help those with mental illness. For example, receiving financial rewards for what we do must be done within an ethical framework.

All forms of self-interest are not selfish in the pejorative way that the latter term is often used. Self-care is essential to all physicians but often neglected (Gabbard 1985; Myers and Gabbard 2008). The definition of self-care can be broadened to include time with family and with close personal relationships that allow physicians and psychiatrists to feel that their own needs are being met so that they have the energy, empathy, and compassion necessary to take care of others. Hence, in addition to a commitment to the altruistic pursuit of taking care of one's patients, psychiatrists need to make a commitment to self-care as well.

The balancing of altruism and self-care is a task of extraordinary complexity, in part because countertransference is an ever-present part of the psychiatrist's practice. Thus a further commitment needs to be made to track one's own countertransference manifestations as they appear in the course of one's practice. Because none of us can observe ourselves with objectivity, the use of supervisors and consultants is essential at various times in one's career, but certainly when one is going through training. Finally, lifelong learning to improve one's knowledge and grasp of the field must be part of the identity of the professional. In this chapter we examine all of these professionalism commitments—altruism, self-care, monitoring one's countertransference, use of supervision and consultation, and lifelong learning—and offer perspectives on how these commitments can be maintained.

Altruism in Psychiatric Practice

Altruism is often defined as emphasizing regard for others in one's choice of action or behavior. The concept of altruism has had to struggle against skepticism from both the evolutionary and psychodynamic perspectives. The view of human nature as an outgrowth of *Homo Beastialis* exerts a powerful influence. Dawkins (1976) noted that if one would like to build a society in which people behaved unselfishly toward a common good, "You can expect little help from biological nature. Let us try to teach generosity and altruism, because we are born selfish" (p. 3). Psychodynamic thought has viewed altruistic behavior as a defense mechanism designed to manage the vicissitudes of instinctual gratification. Vaillant (1992) regarded altruism as a mature defense mechanism and distinguished it from reaction formation in that it redirects the satisfaction of drives instead of opposing it. Hence even psychoanalytic thinking has attempted to "explain away" altruistic behavior as a defensive strategy designed to deal with the fundamental selfish motives in all of us.

An extensive body of research from ethology, experimental psychology, infant studies, and sociobiology suggests that the actual picture of altruism is far more complex (Shapiro and Gabbard 1994). This research suggests that self-oriented and altruistic motivations are inextricably intertwined in the course of development, and both form the basis of complex social behavior patterns. Pure altruism and pure selfishness are most likely convenient abstractions that exist for the purpose of argument. Evolutionary progress demands both other-directed and self-directed motivations. Indeed, both promotion of genetic survival and development of civilized society depend on cooperative and altruistic strategies.

A more enlightened definition of *altruism* is that it describes behavior or motivation designed to meet the needs of others that is not limited to motivation for personal gain or self-interest. Within this context, altruism may be in part defensive but may have other motives as well. A corollary arising from this definition is that the same act may be self-centered or altruistic, depending on the most consciously available and predominant motivation of the individual performing the act. A person walking on a bridge over a river may witness a child falling into freezing waters. One person may leap into the water with a conscious motivation of saving the child from drowning. Another person might hesitate but then change his mind, thinking it might be good for his reputation to appear on the evening news as a hero. Both may save the child, but with different motivations. In this example, we focus on conscious motivations, knowing that selfish and altruistic goals commonly coexist in a particular choice of actions. In keeping with the core psychodynamic principle of overdetermination of symptoms, fantasies, and behaviors, generally we would find a multilayered set of conscious and unconscious motivations that converge to produce one's specific behavior. If a religious individual performs a good deed, there may be a mixture of motivations involving a genuine wish to help others, a tormenting superego demanding that he conform to parental values, a wish to be recognized by others as a good Christian, and a desire to assure his place in heaven.

Recent research suggests that we may actually be genetically programmed to feel rewarded as a result of altruism. Researchers at the University of Oregon (Harbaugh et al. 2007) conducted a study in which 19 students were given $100 each and told that they had the option of donating some of the money to charity anonymously. The students who donated the highest percentage of their money activated pleasure centers in their brain. Hence generosity was rewarded. However, two of the students who were most generous showed no neural reward on the scanning done in the research, suggesting that altruism may be motivated by other factors besides the activation of pleasure centers. One can speculate, of course, that differences in internalized value systems set in childhood are responsible for the varying degree of neural reward associated with generosity.

The Balance Between Self-Care and Altruism

Individuals who are successful in gaining admission to medical school tend to be highly compulsive and conscientious students who "run the extra mile" to ensure that everything is done as near to perfection as possible (Gabbard 1985; Myers and Gabbard 2008). Whatever compulsive and perfectionistic traits they may have prior to medical school are certainly exacerbated as a result of the acculturation to academic medical training cultures. Senior professors may teach that self-sacrifice in the interest of the patient is not only laudable but essential. Role models may appear at 5:00 in the morning for rounds and be seen leaving the medical center at 10:00 or 11:00 at night. This neglect of self-care and intimate relationships may be powerfully reinforced by the training setting itself. A prospective study of 421 Norwegian (Tyssen et al. 2007) medical students found that particular personality traits, especially neuroticism and conscientiousness, were independent predictors of stress among medical students. They identified a "brooder" subtype who is more likely to worry than a subtype referred to as the "hedonist," who scores lower on neuroticism and conscientiousness.

The same group examined levels of stress related to work-home interference and found that it was particularly problematic during one's early career after training. The level of stress related to balancing family and work significantly increased compared with what it was during the training. Long-standing stress from the work-home interface has been shown to relate to deterioration of physician health (Linzer et al. 2001). In the Norwegian sample, spouse support seemed to be an important protective variable (Røvik et al. 2007). However, spouse support may vary directly with the young physician's capacity to value time with family and other important personal relationships. In many cases, the need to work trumps family or personal concerns (Gabbard and Menninger 1989).

Extensive studies of physician-in-training and physician health conducted over the past 30 years demonstrate that doctors are not immune to physical and mental health concerns. In a study of 1,027 medical students at nine medical schools, Roberts et al. (2001) found that 95% of the medical students had needed healthcare, with 19% requiring overnight hospitalization, over the 4 years of undergraduate medical training. Nearly half (47%) of the students needing care had at least one stress-related, mental health, or substance-related issue, ranging from relationship discord to prescription drug abuse. A significant proportion of students at every school reported that they had encountered difficulty getting healthcare (too busy, worried about cost, lack of access, confidentiality worries). Overall 63% of students in the study had sought informal or "curbside" consultation, "off the books" so to speak, in order to get their health needs met. Perhaps one reason for seeking informal care was the finding that students expressed concern that their academic status would be jeopardized if they became ill. The greatest fear was expressed regarding stigmatized conditions such as drug, alcohol, or medication abuse, HIV and sexually transmitted infections, and depression, anxiety, and eating disorders. Still, students feared that having arthritis, diabetes, peptic ulcer disease, or a complicated pregnancy would still create academic jeopardy, were it to be known by "the dean's office." A subsequent study of residents indicated that these same health needs, care-seeking practices, and fears continue and may amplify over the course of advanced training (Dunn et al. 2009).

In another study (Dunn et al. 2009), primary care and specialty residents commonly indicated that they personally had seen other residents postpone or avoid seeking healthcare, with the reasons most often cited as concerns about privacy and fear that a supervisor might "find out." They also more frequently endorsed that residents were "ostracized" and criticized rather than empathized with when they became ill and had to miss work. Again in this study, addiction (prescription medication, other drugs, alcohol), sexually transmitted disease, and mental health issues generated the greatest concern for stigma. Women and specialty residents were especially sensitive to stigma in this study. Taken together, this line of empirical work suggests that physicians have healthcare needs but adopt poor self-care practices early in their professional lives.

It is important to see this phenomenon as an opportunity, however, because the personal experience of caring for one's health and of becoming ill has profound positive effects. Physicians who have strong personal self-care and an orientation toward preventive health in their own lives tend to carry this same philosophy into their work with patients. Many courageous physicians have also written about the empathy that is inspired by living, and at times dying, with an illness. The brilliant gastroenterologist Franz Ingelfinger (1980) wrote about the wisdom he gained regarding the role of empathy in medicine, not through many years of clinical practice but in the short time he lived with cancer of the liver before he died.

Psychiatrists may in some ways be typical of physicians, whereas in other ways they are different. We concur with Louie et al. (2007), who wrote:

> Physicians are prone to overworking. Diverse factors contribute to this result, including the medical school selection process and a professional ethic that embraces hard work, excessive service demands, and fiduciary obligations to patients.... Psychiatrists, in particular, are vulnerable to occupational stress when working with emotional and behavioral disorders. Ours is an emotionally demanding profession. Among physicians, psychiatrists represent a group predisposed to career exhaustion.... The divorced rate is also higher for psychiatrists than physicians in other subspecialties...(and) unique to psychiatry, threats or assault by a patient and suicide are the most stressful adversities encountered in training. (p. 129)

We have much less prospective data on the personality traits of psychiatrists that lead to having an increase in stress or in neglecting self-care. However, from the psychodynamic perspective, we can assume that the balance of altruism versus self-interest may be related to genetic factors, such as a temperament high in neuroticism as well as early experiences that lead to patterns of internalized object relations that play out in relationships with others. Work as a psychiatrist will be affected by imbalance in one direction or another and will play out in the capacity to function as a professional. Psychiatrists whose primary motivation involves narcissistic gratification or self-interest may find it difficult to empathize with the distress experienced by patients. They may be more concerned with seeing as many "med check" patients as possible in 1 hour to enhance their wealth or with relating to their patients in such a way as to maximize an idealized transference that buffers them against feelings of insecurity.

If the imbalance occurs in the opposite direction, these psychiatrists may sacrifice their own needs and enslave themselves masochistically to their patients as a result of excessive guilt feelings and an exaggerated sense of responsibility toward the patient (Gabbard 1985; Shapiro and Gabbard 1994). Psychiatrists who are excessively altruistic therapists may be compulsive "rescuers" who deny their own needs in a way that is just as destructive as a pattern of unchecked gratification. These patterns of interaction with patients may represent reaction formation more than altruism in that they are trying to convince themselves that they do not harbor feelings of sadism, hatred, and aggression. By tirelessly helping others, they may be unconsciously reassuring themselves that they are not acting on aggressive feelings but clearly devoting themselves to others. These types of psychiatrists may predispose themselves to forms of boundary violations as a way of proving to the patient that they care when confronted with overt aggression in the transference (Gabbard and Lester 2003).

> Dr. Appleton, a 36-year-old psychiatrist and mother of two, was treating a chronically suicidal patient with borderline personality disorder using combined medication and psychotherapy. She had regularly received calls in the middle of the night in which she would listen to her patient talk about suicidal impulses. Dr. Appleton felt concerned that the patient was at substantial risk for actually attempting suicide, and she knew the patient refused to go to the hospital under such circumstances. Hence she would stay on the phone, sometimes for an hour at a time, and lose substantial sleep.
>
> This pattern made it difficult for her to get up in the morning and get to work on time, and it complicated the morning routine; her husband felt unduly burdened in getting the kids ready because she was exhausted from being up much of the night. One day after she had talked with the patient on the phone at length during the night, she fell asleep during a therapy session with a different patient during the following day. The patient woke her up and told her that maybe he should leave because she was not able to stay alert and listen to his concerns. She assured him that she *was* capable of listening, but he left anyway. Dr. Appleton felt awful and irresponsible. She went next door and talked with her office mate about what had happened. Her office mate suggested that by staying up so late talking with her patient in the middle of the night, she actually was compromising the care of her other patients during the day. She suggested that she start setting limits on the phone calls. Dr. Appleton responded that if she set limits, the patient might kill herself. Her office mate responded that there were hospitals available for suicidal patients and that Dr. Appleton could admit the patient to one of those hospitals if necessary. Dr. Appleton then responded that her patient was unwilling to go to the hospital. Her office mate asked her, "Who is in charge of this treatment plan?"
>
> This interaction made Dr. Appleton aware that in effect, she was allowing herself to be controlled and bullied by the patient, and her altruistic self-sacrifice was actually resulting in harm to her family relationships and to other patients during the day. She had a frank discussion in her next appointment with her chronically suicidal patient in which she said that she was unable to continue to take calls in the middle of the night because she could not function during the day. She explained to

the patient that she had limits and was unable to be continually available. She said that to continue the treatment, the patient would have to channel her concerns about suicide into the regularly scheduled sessions. She also emphasized that if the patient felt overwhelmed with imminent suicidal impulses, she might have to go into the hospital even though it was not her choice.

This example with Dr. Appleton illustrates how the altruistic efforts to rescue a patient may ultimately result in harmful or compromised behavior to other patients as well as neglect of one's self and family. Self-care is intimately linked to professional care of others. Beginning psychiatrists who do not learn these facts of practice early in their careers predispose themselves to mid-career burnout, not to mention the risk of dissatisfied patients, lawsuits, and boundary violations (Spickard et al. 2002). Dr. Appleton's dilemma is one that is readily recognizable by most psychiatrists and psychiatric residents. There is a constant internal pull to be available for a patient and save that patient from suicide, accompanied by feelings of neglect and guilt when one responds to one's own needs instead.

Much of this dilemma has crystallized around work-hour regulations for psychiatric residents. In July 2003, the Accreditation Council for Graduate Medical Education stipulated that residents could work no more than 80 hours per week nor more than 24 consecutive duty hours at a time. The stipulations also involve no more than 12-hour shifts in the emergency department and 24 hours off every 7 days (Rabjohn and Yager 2008). There have been a variety of responses to concerns that professionalism may suffer as a result of these work-hour regulations. Some have felt that being a professional requires one to do what is necessary until a particular unit of work with a specific patient is completed. A sense of ownership of clinical responsibility is critical for professionalism, in this view. Many psychiatric residents feel an ethical dilemma when regulations demand that they must leave while a patient is still requiring care. Both educators and residents have felt to some extent that the need to comply with the rules may supersede a sense of professional commitment to the patient. Nevertheless, most faculty and trainees realize that a resident who is rested and tending to matters at home will ultimately give better care at work. These work-hour regulations have also promoted the notion that handing off care to other professionals may be the wave of the future rather than the old-style commitment to follow a patient's care through to the end of the unit of work.

Self-report data and observational studies suggest that medical students and residents become exhausted physically and emotionally, and many en-

counter abuse and mistreatment during the course of their professional training. From a professionalism perspective, being traumatized in one's training
may establish a harsh and reductionistic psychological perspective in which
colleagues, supervisors, and even patients are being viewed as "aggressors"
who "dump on" the exhausted trainee. Empathy and compassion, essential
to professionalism, are hard to generate in such a milieu.

This threat to professionalism may be lessened through the work-hours
regulations, and yet there appears to be a new issue that many suggest may
undermine the professionalism of medicine. This is the "Generation X" issue. Data from the past decade suggest that the driven need to sacrifice
oneself for one's patients is shifting a bit in terms of medical student decision making. Dorsey et al. (2003) found that controllable lifestyle ac-
counted for more than 55% of the variance in the specialty choice of medical students from 1996–2002. The American College of Physicians has been
concerned that there is a potential for primary care to collapse. Indeed, a
2007 survey showed that 59% of family physicians would choose a different
career path if they had it to do over again (Brewer 2008).

Monitoring Countertransference

In Chapters 1 and 2 we noted that psychiatry is held to a higher standard
because self-reflection on our own emotional reactions to our patients is expected as part of our clinical expertise. Other specialties do not emphasize
the fact that physicians are constantly enacting unconscious conflicts, wishes,
and biases in their everyday interactions with patients. Hence another
professionalism commitment is to systematically examine how the patient
influences our thoughts and feelings as well as how we are correspondingly
influencing the patient.

> Dr. Hanson was a 29-year-old fellow who was in his second year of training
> to be a child psychiatrist. Freddy was a 14-year-old patient who was sent
> to see him by his parents because he was sullen around the house and
> outright defiant when his parents tried to impose structure on him or
> exert any kind of discipline. He was similarly rebellious and oppositional
> toward his teachers at school. Nevertheless, he was making reasonably
> good grades and attending class. His parents were frankly perplexed about

why he had a chip on his shoulder and did not know what to do, so they brought him to psychotherapy. They told Dr. Hanson that they had tried on numerous occasions to discuss the problems Freddy was having with them, but he spent all his time at the computer and would only half-heartedly attend to what they were saying.

Dr. Hanson started seeing Freddy at 5:00 on Wednesday evenings after school. Freddy came into the office, said hello, and then took out his homework and worked on it while Dr. Hanson sat and asked questions. Dr. Hanson asked him why he was doing homework during therapy. Freddy responded, "I really don't have anything to talk about, and I have to get this homework done, so it's a lot better than just wasting time." Dr. Hanson replied, "Isn't anything bothering you?" Freddy thought for a moment, then clarified, "The only thing bothering me is that my parents make me come here." Hence much of the time in therapy was passed in silence while Freddy continued to do his homework and rarely made eye contact with Dr. Hanson. Dr. Hanson noted an increasing irritation at Freddy's contempt toward him, and he dreaded the sessions. Nevertheless, he felt he must provide a different kind of parental experience that would be corrective for Freddy. Hence he did not demand that Freddy put his books aside, nor did he demand that Freddy speak with him.

One Wednesday, 3 months into the therapy, one of Dr. Hanson's old friends asked him if he could go to dinner with him on Wednesday evening, and Dr. Hanson left a few minutes before 5:00 to meet his friend. At 10 minutes after 5, when he was driving to the dinner, he suddenly realized that he'd totally forgotten that he had an appointment with Freddy at 5. He frantically called the child clinic where he worked and asked the receptionist to tell Freddy that he'd be a little bit late. He then called his friend and cancelled the dinner, apologizing profusely. When Dr. Hanson got back to the clinic at 5:25, he told Freddy to come into his office and apologized for running late.

Freddy had been doing his homework in the waiting room, and he simply picked up his notebook and textbook and continued the homework when he got into Dr. Hanson's office. Freddy said, "So you forgot about me today," never looking up from his notebook.

Dr. Hanson replied, "No, I didn't forget about you. I just got held up elsewhere." He immediately felt a twinge of guilt, recognizing that he was being dishonest to cover up what he viewed as his lack of professionalism and irresponsibility. Freddy laughed contemptuously in response to Dr. Hanson's lame excuse. Dr. Hanson blushed crimson as he sat watching Freddy do his homework, and he realized that he really could not stand Freddy. He thought to himself that he was becoming a psychiatrist to help people and give children a chance to understand themselves and feel validated in a therapeutic relationship. Freddy was not participating in that fantasy of what child psychiatrists were supposed to do, and Dr. Hanson deeply resented it. As he sat with his feelings, he also recognized that he was becoming just as desperate as Freddy's parents in that he could not make him do anything. Just as Freddy's mother and father were throwing up their hands in despair and seeking out a psychiatrist for advice, Dr. Hanson himself was now feeling that the therapy was futile and wondering if he should transfer the patient to someone else. It suddenly dawned on him that he had fallen into the same relational paradigm in which Freddy and his parents were stuck.

Dr. Hanson had started psychotherapy for himself 6 months prior to the beginning of his therapy with Freddy, and he had spoken about his growing feelings of helplessness and anger in the face of Freddy's noncompliance with treatment. As he sat there feeling humiliated by his countertransference enactment, Dr. Hanson remembered something that his therapist had said: "One of the things you're struggling with is that you need your patients to respond to you in a certain way to make you feel good about yourself. Unfortunately, your patients will be who they are rather than respond to your needs." Dr. Hanson recognized on further self-reflection that he "forgot" about Freddy's appointment because he did not want to be reminded of how little he mattered to Freddy and face the feelings of shame, impotence, and boredom associated with sitting silently while Freddy did his homework. It made him feel like a fool.

In this example, Dr. Hanson is learning the groundwork for a lifelong commitment to monitor his countertransference. This particular experience with Freddy is illustrative of how countertransference generally involves some issues that are induced by the behavior of the patient as well as subjective contributions from the psychiatrist himself (Gabbard 2010). Freddy treats Dr. Hanson with the same disdain that he treats his own parents. Hence the interpersonal pressure placed on Dr. Hanson by Freddy's absorption in his own homework and obliviousness to the therapist makes Dr. Hanson feel helpless and exasperated, just as Freddy's parents feel. This model of countertransference is an example of *projective identification,* in which Dr. Hanson identifies with what has been projected into him unconsciously by Freddy.

However, Freddy does not simply project into a vacuum. Dr. Hanson brings his own past to the consulting room, along with his own aspirations, fantasies, and needs for validation. He begins to recognize that Freddy is a master at making him feel useless. He knows from his own psychotherapy that he has a longstanding need and desire to make an impact in a useful way on children and adolescents to undo some experiences from his own childhood. He often felt he had no impact on his father, who would sit and read the newspaper when Dr. Hanson wanted to speak with him. As he went on to explore his countertransference in psychotherapy, he began to realize that in some way he also had recreated a problem from his past—namely, that he was trying to communicate and connect with someone who was oblivious to his presence. Freddy had become a version of Dr. Hanson's father in the ongoing enactments of the therapy. In this regard, Dr. Hanson had a convenient "hook" for Freddy's projections. The two were unconsciously engaging in a dance that sustained a pattern jointly constructed with elements from both of their lives. Dr. Hanson became aware of this countertransference because he enacted it. Countertransference is initially unconscious, and it may only be through enactments that the therapist begins to become fully aware of the nature of the countertransference (Gabbard 1995).

This professionalism commitment to self-awareness and to examining one's own contributions to the treatment relationship transcends the work of psychiatrists who are psychotherapists. In psychiatric inpatient units, in consultation-liaison work, and in medication management, countertransference issues are just as significant. Psychiatrists may find themselves adding one medication after another to the patient's treatment plan when they feel exasperated at the patient for not getting better. They may prescribe benzodiazepines in high quantities to a patient because they fear the patient's anger and resentment if they do not comply with the patient's request. They may suggest electroconvulsive therapy for a depressed patient even before exhausting all the possible antidepressant combinations because of an unconscious wish to punish or "zap" the patient with shock rather than listen to the patient's complaints. They may discharge the patient prematurely because they do not want to treat the patient. They may prolong a patient's stay in the hospital because they have extremely positive feelings and enjoy their interactions with the patient.

Whatever the nature of a psychiatrist's practice, self-awareness is of great importance. Because of this unique feature of psychiatry, many psychiatrists choose to enter psychotherapy or psychoanalysis either as a trainee or later in life when different issues involved in different developmental phases arise. Another professionalism commitment is for the psychiatrist to seek out help, swallowing any sense of wounded pride or humiliation, when they need to have a good look at themselves. Recognizing that we are all imperfect, all vulnerable, and all heir to the weaknesses of the flesh is a fundamental component to self-care.

Supervision and Consultation

Another professionalism commitment involves avoiding professional isolation. Psychiatrists cannot see themselves as others see them, and they cannot detect every countertransference enactment from their own perspective. For this reason, psychiatrists need to commit themselves to seeking out consultation and supervision when necessary throughout their professional lives. Psychiatrists are trained in a triad: patient, resident, and supervisor. When they finish their residency, there is often a sense of freedom to try their own wings and fly solo. For most of the psychiatrist's practice, this self-reliance does not create difficulty, but each of us has a set of vulnerabilities that are triggered by particular patients in certain situations that "push one's buttons." Because of this human condition, all psychiatrists need to have some form of consultative situation in which they can speak freely about their concerns and receive the wisdom of another perspective from a valued colleague. Someone outside us sees things about us that we do not see ourselves.

Supervision has an evaluative function during psychiatric residency training, and the psychiatric resident has to come to grips with the realization that excessive concern about one's performance evaluation can undermine the whole point of supervision. In other words, if the resident is not forthright about the concerns in the psychotherapy, the educational value of the supervision is greatly compromised. Hence, as noted in Chapter 3, residents in supervision, like psychiatrists in consultation, must make a commitment to "tell it like it is." They need to express their concerns about errors, their desires for the patient, their hatred of the patient, and their departures from usual practice. The aspects of the treatment that they most wish to conceal from the supervisor are the very issues they should be bringing up. Most supervisors will respect the honesty of the supervisee who has the courage to give an accurate account of his or her struggles. No supervisor expects the resident to have mastered psychotherapy or other forms of clinical practice during the brief time he or she is in residency. Years of experience are necessary to gain that sense of mastery.

After graduating from a training program, psychiatrists may find many excuses for not seeking consultation. They can argue that it is too expensive, that it is too inconvenient, that no one else can understand the complexities of the treatment with a particular patient, that they do not have time in their busy schedule, and that they should be able to solve problems for themselves. They also may feel guilty about the kind of treatment they are doing or about their lack of knowledge about particular treatments. To many, consultation involves exposure of potential weaknesses. Nevertheless, part of being a professional is the commitment to constantly improve one's craft. So psychiatrists must find a way to connect with others and to learn from them.

One-to-one consultation on a periodic basis is obviously only one model. Some psychiatrists prefer to meet in groups on a regular basis for dinner, lunch, or breakfast and share their struggles with one another. Over time, a sense of familiarity and safety develops in the group so that each person can be open about his or her struggles. In this way, the consultation is reciprocal, and one person is not always in a "one up" position over the other. Other psychiatrists feel more comfortable seeking out a senior colleague in a mentoring role so that there is a clear understanding that one person is helping the other without the expectation of reciprocity.

There are myriad ways that one can undermine consultation so that it is of minimal value. Psychiatrists may catch a colleague in the hallway, at a professional meeting, over the coffeepot, or at a social event to obtain a "curbside" consultation. In that context, the psychiatrist can ask a question with the expectation of a brief confirming response so that he or she hears the desired answer. A colleague may catch another colleague off guard and say, "Have you felt that sometimes a patient really needs a hug, and it really does no damage to the process?" In an offhand way, the colleague may respond in the affirmative, and the consultee can reassure her or himself that no harm has been done and continue to hug the patient on a regular basis. Similarly, a consultee may conceal certain aspects of the treatment so the consultant has a partial picture and thus cannot give a truly useful consultation.

Another component of self-care is not subjecting oneself to the impossible situation of trying to figure out all problems that come up in clinical practice on one's own. Seeking help from others when necessary is a way of taking care of oneself. Commitment to consultation is a commitment to the self.

Lifelong Learning

Consultation is one part of lifelong learning that is essential for all psychiatrists. The general public expects all physicians to maintain knowledge of current advances in the field. Psychiatrists also have a professionalism commitment that involves reading journals and books, attending meetings, going to continuing education courses, and maintaining recertification as needed.

Most psychiatrists end up developing various kinds of subspecialties, either formally through subspecialty training or informally through practice and interest. One of the other aspects of lifelong learning is recognizing one's limits and realizing what one is not learning as a result of one's area of interest, so the psychiatrist can supplement lack of experience with knowledge about innovations for disorders that may be seen only rarely in one's practice. A corollary of this point is that one must not attempt treatments where one lacks the requisite training and experience to be competent. Especially when times are difficult from an economic perspective, some psychiatrists are tempted to expand into areas where they are really not knowledgeable. A part of one's commitment to put the patient's needs before the psychiatrist's needs is to avoid promoting oneself as a practitioner for all seasons.

Conclusion

Balancing self-care and altruism is a lifelong task that is never accomplished in any perfect manner. In a similar vein, balancing work and family matters is equally messy. We try to approximate these balancing acts with the notion that being "good enough" is the goal—not perfection.

One quick way of assessing your commitment to self-care is by doing a simple exercise (Gabbard and Menninger 1989; Myers and Gabbard 2008). Write out the five highest priorities in your life when no one is looking so that you know you are being honest. Then compare these priorities to your schedule book from the past week. See how much time you devote to those things that matter the most. The results may be highly disconcerting, but they may help you reassess priorities.

Key Points

- An altruistic commitment to help others who are suffering, even when it may be inconvenient for the physician, is inherent to medicine and psychiatry.

- *Altruism* describes behavior or motivation designed to meet the needs of others that is not limited to motivation for personal gain or self-interest.

- A critical and complex task is balancing healthy self-interest with altruism.

- Physicians and medical students have physical and mental healthcare needs during training but often adopt poor self-care practices early in their professional lives.

- Psychiatrists in particular are vulnerable to occupational stress. They may need to pay particular attention to the tendency to neglect self-care when faced with countertransference feelings of narcissistic gratification, the idealized transferences of patients, rescue fantasies, and reaction formation against hatred or aggression in themselves or in their patients.

- Because countertransference is often unconscious, at least initially, an enactment may be one of the first clues to awareness of the particular ways that the therapist is reacting to the patient's projections. Self-awareness is of critical importance for psychiatrists, and a decision for psychiatrists to enter their own psychotherapy may be important for them to develop self-awareness of their own vulnerabilities and imperfections.

- Supervision and consultation are essential during training and important tools to be used subsequently to avoid isolation. These practices used regularly and when necessary can help us to see ourselves and our clinical work with patients in ways that we cannot see unassisted.

- The education that one begins during residency cannot stop after training, and lifelong learning must continue to establish an ongoing foundation for these practices.

Chapter 6

Sensitivity to Culture, Race, Gender, and Sexual Orientation

Psychiatry involves values-based decisions of profound importance in the lives of patients. The work is not formulaic or strictly rule based. There is accommodation in the encounter between the physician and the patient, and there are specific contexts in which this encounter occurs. The meanings that illness takes on in the unfolding life story of the patient are influenced by that patient's sense of gender, racial/ethnic background, cultural/religious heritage, and sexual orientation. The doctor-patient interaction occurs in a community context and a clinical care setting that have their own characteristics as well. Mental health professionals caring for patients also bring their own gender, race, culture, sexual orientation, and religious backgrounds to the interaction. All of these elements shape the values operative in the psychiatrist-patient encounter.

Throughout one's career a repeated challenge is the task of empathizing with and understanding those who are different than oneself. Patients who are different in terms of their ethnicity, gender, or belief systems represent the "other" in the unconscious of the psychiatrist—someone who is "not like me." An ongoing challenge in the sphere of professionalism

91

is for psychiatrists to build an empathic bridge to someone who is different, to make a genuine effort to understand someone who has characteristics that are alien to one's own. Psychiatrists must go beyond cultural *tolerance* to strive for cultural *empathy*. Tolerance is too easily equated with "putting up" with someone else's beliefs even though you really believe that the way YOU see things is superior. Cultural empathy implies a process of immersing yourself in someone else's experience and attempting to view things in the way the "Other" sees the world.

One must be attuned to what Freud (1918) called the "narcissism of minor differences." Freud noted that we tend to overfocus on very small differences between ourselves and others to make ourselves feel superior in some way:

> It is precisely the minor differences in people who are otherwise alike that form the basis of feelings of strangeness and hostility between them. It would be tempting to pursue this idea and to derive from this "narcissism of minor differences" the hostility which in every human relation we see fighting successfully against feelings of fellowship and overpowering the commandment that all men should love one another. (p. 199)

Freud (1921) went on to apply this thinking to the way people in neighboring countries regarded those on the other side of the border, and he recognized this form of narcissism as a universal human characteristic:

> In the undisguised antipathies and aversions which people feel towards strangers with whom they have to do we may recognize the expression of self-love—of narcissism. This self-love works for the preservation of the individual, and behaves as though the occurrence of any divergence from his own particular lines of development involved a criticism of them and a demand for their alteration. We do not know why such sensitiveness should have been directed to just these details of differentiation; but it is unmistakable that in this whole connection men give evidence of a readiness for hatred, an aggressiveness, the source of which is unknown, and to which one is tempted to ascribe an elementary character. (p. 102)

Clearly this phenomenon is involved in prejudice and intolerance of those who are different than ourselves. It can also be applied to the minor differences of gender (Gabbard 1993).

Mental health professionals must be aware of this tendency in all of us and recognize that it may be inevitable that we tend to disparage those with differences unless we make a conscious effort to understand their perspective and appreciate the value in heritages and traditions that are foreign to us. In this chapter we consider in broad terms the professionalism challenges that are inherent in relating to those who are of opposite gender, of different cultures, of racial/ethnic origins that are distinct from our own, and of different sexual orientation. We also comment on particular difficulties that sometimes arise with patients who have *similar* cultural and/or ethnic origins.

Cultural Competence and Professionalism

Culture is a concept that defies facile definition. To ask a patient to describe his or her culture is like asking a fish to describe water. It is the very fabric of the patient's existence, and there may be little self-awareness of its influence. Culture is certainly learned rather than intrinsic and involves a complex system of meanings (Gaw 1993). Tseng and Streltzer (2004) defined it as "the unique behavior patterns and lifestyle shared by a group of people that distinguish it from other groups. A culture is characterized by a set of views, beliefs, values, and attitudes…manifested in…various ways in which life is regulated, such as rituals, customs, etiquette, taboos and laws" (Tseng and Streltzer 2004, p. 1). They also noted that there is an ongoing reciprocal influence of culture and people.

When we apply culture to psychiatric encounters, we must acknowledge that the order of complexity substantially increases. We have patient-related aspects, clinician-related aspects, and context-related aspects. Moreover, we have no reason to believe that each of these entities is constituted by one pure culture. Both patients and psychiatrists can be influenced by a mix of cultures. The setting can similarly be a mosaic of cultural influences. Finally, so often religious and spiritual belief systems are embedded in culture. When we attempt to achieve cultural competence as part of our aspirations toward professionalism, we speak of different models. One is cultural awareness and sensitivity, which essentially involves the conscientious effort to see each patient as growing up in a specific cultural context that must be taken into account as we develop a formulation of the patient that is truly biopsychosociocultural in its comprehensiveness. Another model noted at the beginning of this chapter can be conceptualized as cultural empathy, which involves the authentic appreciation of the experience of the patient from another path dissimilar to one's own. This attempt to mentalize the other person's inner and outer world is a fundamental skill that psychiatrists must develop to be good clinicians. One must transcend one's own biases and narcissism to see the other person's perspective without excessive judgment or thinly disguised contempt. A third model is straightforward—we must acquire cultural knowledge of a particular cultural heritage to be competent. When that is lacking with a specific patient, we may need to ask the patient to educate us in the course of the treatment relationship, but we may also choose to read appropriate references so that we can better attune ourselves to the relevant issues of the patient.

> A Native American patient who was an elder in his Navajo tribe was in a state of sepsis due to an untreated infection. He was a long-standing diabetic who was approaching end-state illness. The surgeons managing his case consulted a psychiatrist in the consultation-liaison division of the hospital. They explained that the patient was refusing amputation of his foot even though it was essential to save the patient's life. The psychiatrist met with the patient and explored the meaning of the amputation within the Navajo man's culture. She learned that his culture held a strong belief that the body must be complete at the time of burial. When the psychiatrist learned that it would be possible to preserve the foot and bury it with him when he passed away, the patient accepted the life-preserving intervention of amputation.

Part of cultural competence is also developing a moment-to-moment awareness of the interaction between the psychiatrist's cultural background and the patient's cultural background. Transference is always based on real characteristics that serve as a nidus for the projection of fantasies about the clinician from the patient's unconscious. Similarly, the psychiatrist brings a set of beliefs and biases that stem from his or her own cultural background. These may serve as conscious or unconscious countertransferences that influence the way the psychiatrist diagnoses and treats the patient. Also, patients with particular cultural beliefs may appear to be resisting all of the clinician's help because the belief system of the psychiatrist (e.g., scientific method) is at odds with the beliefs of the patient. One patient of Hispanic and Apache descent did not adhere to the treatment regimen and was regarded as a "difficult" patient. When a culturally competent psychiatrist made the effort to understand the sources of the resistance, he learned that the man believed that mental illness derived from being out of balance with the harmony of nature because he lived in an urban setting. The treatment team found it necessary to link their treatment regimen with a Native American healer who used a complementary approach. In other words, the team recognized the necessity of culturally informed decision making—that is, seeking to affirm the values derived from the cultural background of the patient.

Why is cultural competence necessary for psychiatric professionalism? Gaw (1993) outlined the rationale succinctly: It enhances accurate diagnosis and facilitates treatment effectiveness. The sensitivity to cultural issues improves attunement with patients and forges a stronger therapeutic alliance. Cultural competence also refines our thinking about stigma, norms, differences, pathology, and deviance, and in so doing expands psychiatric knowledge. Finally, it improves our understanding of the human condition in general as well as the in-depth understanding of a particular individual who consults us for problems.

Cultural competence carries with it a set of risks, however, and these must be taken into account if one is to promote professionalism. We must be sure that we safeguard the patient by taking seriously all clinical data. For example, newly manifested symptoms of illness must not be dismissed as culturally held religious beliefs. Caring for the patient must be first and foremost even when striving for cultural competence. A patient with both a brain tumor and schizoaffective disorder had the culturally congruent psychotic experience of visitation from a dead daughter as he fell asleep at night. Even though this phenomenon could be understood culturally, the psychiatrist treating the patient had the clinical acumen to take appropriate treatment measures.

Another risk is to yield too far in the direction of cultural expectations and transgress ethics boundaries in so doing. For example, in some cultures, the head of the family is entitled to information about the clinical condition faced by a family member. The treating psychiatrist must explain the principle of confidentiality in such situations and consult with the patient regarding the situation. The patient can then decide whether to sign a release of information allowing the doctor to talk to the head of the family. Families may also wish to dictate what is said to the patient, in direct opposition to the doctor's clinical judgment of what is best. One family wanted the psychiatrist treating an impaired elder to describe the medication being prescribed as a "vitamin" rather than an antipsychotic.

A serious risk in attempting to be culturally sensitive is that one can unwittingly promulgate cultural stereotypes. One Hispanic male patient was offended when his psychiatrist suggested that he was somatizing his depression. The patient said, "I don't see this as something in my body at all. I see it as clinical depression. I read about it on the Internet." The psychiatrist had been taught by a Hispanic teacher that many Hispanic men prefer to have a physical illness rather than acknowledge depression. This particular patient, however, did not fit that common cultural phenomenon. Each patient is still an individual with all the uniqueness inherent in that individuality. Cultural values and traditions are accepted to greater or lesser degrees depending on the patient. One has to approach each patient as a person without making erroneous assumptions based on generalizations regarding culture.

Cultural issues are ubiquitous but may initially be invisible. A patient who is the first in his family to attend college and who holds many cherished cultural beliefs may look like, speak like, and share similar socioeconomic status with the clinician. The psychiatrist treating the patient may thus minimize the impact of culture only to be shocked when the patient makes it clear that he is steeped in cultural traditions. One must assume nothing and in each case relate in a compassionate way that facilitates open communication about cultural matters.

Ethnicity and Race

Ethnicity is often differentiated from culture on the basis of its biological component. There are, for example, distinct differences in metabolism of medications and genetic differences in prevalence of disease. Addressing these biological phenomena is also part of culturally competent professionalism. However, we must also recognize that race is largely a social construction. Terms such as "white" and "black" have been applied in an arbitrary fashion throughout history and have been used in highly diverse ways in different epochs and in different populations (Painter 2010). Whiteness, for example, is often code for other phenomena, such as wealth, higher social status, beauty, power, and employment status (Painter 2010).

Unconscious stereotyping has impacted the mental health assessments and evaluations of minorities. Researchers have reported that diagnostic bias has resulted in the overdiagnosis of schizophrenia and the underdiagnosis of affective disorders in African American patients (Adebimpe 1981; Bell and Mehta 1998; Coleman and Baker 1994; Jones et al. 1981). Other studies indicate that when structured clinical interviews, Research

Diagnostic Criteria, or diagnostic criteria from the Schedule for Affective Disorder and Schizophrenia were used, then rates of schizophrenia were more comparable with those of whites (Liss et al. 1973; Simon et al. 1973; Welner et al. 1973). The inaccuracy in making the appropriate diagnoses has been attributed to limited awareness of cultural differences in language and mannerisms and difficulty in establishing rapport between a black patient and white therapist as well as beliefs in the myth that blacks rarely have affective disorders.

A key aspect of professionalism is making oneself aware of the ubiquity of unconscious racism and stereotyping. A substantial body of literature has developed based on this phenomenon. Word et al. (1974) conducted a study at Princeton University that involved simulated job interviews. Princeton students served as interviewers for employment for both black and white interviewees. When the interviewees were African American, the white Princeton students tended to sit farther away from the interviewee, made more errors in their speech, and ended the interviews earlier compared with when they interviewed white interviewees. When the students were instructed to engage in the same types of nonverbal behavior that they demonstrated with black interviewees when interviewing white applicants, the white interviewees developed performance problems that were not previously observed. The results of the study revealed that African Americans applying for jobs could be discriminated against during the interview process despite the fact that interviewers did not consciously maintain discriminatory beliefs about African Americans.

Greenwald et al. (1998) developed a race-implicit association test that is used to evaluate positive or negative associations of black and white faces by using descriptive adjectives. In research involving the test, black and white faces were quickly flashed on a screen. After these images, the subject was instructed to immediately choose an adjective that correlated with the face. Researchers discovered that even when subjects intended to associate positive descriptions with black faces as quickly as they did with white faces, they were unable to do so. Hence even those who believed themselves to be explicitly without racial prejudice could not overcome their unconscious stereotyping, despite their most intense conscious efforts to do so.

Many psychiatric residents will resist training in cultural competence because they feel that they are absolutely open minded toward patients (and colleagues) of other ethnic or racial groups and feel offended at the implication that they are unaware of their unconscious racism. Caucasian trainees, in particular, as members of the majority culture, may be oblivious to the microaggressions and microtraumas (Pierce 1995) that African Americans have inflicted on them on a daily basis—for example, being ignored by cab drivers or being followed by security in a department store. Due to these microaggressions and history of injustices in the medical profession, many minority patients have developed a "healthy mistrust" of the healthcare system. Therefore, some blacks develop a negative institutional transference toward the healthcare system that is often projected onto a white therapist. For example, the Tuskegee syphilis study (Gray 1998) was a clinical study conducted from 1932 to 1972 in Tuskegee, Alabama. During this period, investigators recruited 399 impoverished sharecroppers with syphilis for research. The study led to intense controversy because researchers failed to treat these patients after the development of penicillin as an effective cure for syphilis. The patients were observed so that researchers could evaluate the natural progression of untreated illness. The outrage in response to this project led to the first U.S. legislative changes geared toward the protection of participants in clinical trials (e.g., informed consent). Consequently, understanding the historical framework of the spread of racism into the medical field will increase the likelihood for better cultural sensitivity and thereby improve professional standards of care.

One common barrier to cultural sensitivity is limited awareness of others' cultural experiences. For instance, certain racial experiences may be largely invisible to white trainees because of what is commonly referred to as "white privilege,"—that is, their upbringing may have shielded them from the slings and arrows of racial prejudice. Hence there may be acute sensitivity about this legacy of shameful superiority in white trainees, resulting in white guilt. In some white trainees there may be a tendency to distance oneself from any current propensities to view ethnic and racial minorities with stereotypic views widely held by the society at large. Race-related issues may surface in the discourse despite these efforts. Professionalism, as well as good clinical technique, demands that no issue can be off limits in a therapeutic relationship. The sensitive clinician needs to address these racial and ethnic concerns with tact, courage, and professionalism.

> Mr. Palmer, an African American professional man, was seeing Dr. Stinson, a white psychiatrist, for symptoms of depression. During one session, he made reference to being stopped in his own neighborhood by a patrol car while walking his dog. He said in passing to Dr. Stinson, "Oh well,

you wouldn't get what that's like for a black man." He then went on to change the subject. Dr. Stinson interrupted and said, "Of course I get what that's like. It's outrageous!" Mr. Palmer paused and said, "You think you get it, but you really don't unless you're black. You're a good therapist, but there are some things that you can't fully appreciate about me." Dr. Stinson was taken aback by the patient's response—he felt hurt and defensive. He wanted to argue with the accusation that he did not understand racism. He chose to restrain himself and reflect for a moment because there was an irreducible truth about the limits of empathy that Mr. Palmer was pointing out to him. He finally acknowledged, "I suppose you're right. There are some things I need to learn through your eyes."

In this exchange, the therapist's effort to support Mr. Palmer backfired. He wanted to assure his patient that he was on his side and similarly outraged by the incident with the police, but his empathy rang hollow. He realized after the confrontation from his patient that he would need to learn more from his patient about what it is like to experience racial discrimination. Subsequently, he repaired the offense of the patient by acknowledging that he was limited in his awareness of the patient's cultural experience. This is an exemplary illustration of managing one's own lapse in cultural understanding.

There are also moments in the clinician's career in which he or she will encounter overt racism from a patient. When the patient offends the treater in the therapeutic encounter, it is critical to maintain a professional approach despite the affront.

Mrs. Goldsmith, a 70-year-old Caucasian woman with severe refractory major depressive disorder and borderline personality disorder, was admitted to an inpatient setting. She was introduced to her new doctor, Dr. Miller, a young African American psychiatric resident. The patient informed the doctor that she must be mistaken and refused to engage the resident in discussion. She maintained limited interaction with her and dismissed the resident's attempt to engage her throughout the hospital course. The patient had to be readmitted several days after discharge secondary to a serious suicide attempt and was again assigned to the resident's care. The following exchange took place:

"Where is my doctor?" she asked. "I am not talking to anyone else but my doctor." The resident replied, "I am the doctor on call for the evening and the attending physician is unavailable." The patient retorted, "Well, I will just wait right here until he can come." The resident explained that he would not return to the hospital until the next morning. The patient angrily replied, "Well, I will just spend the night in the emergency room then." At that time, the resident felt that this was the time to uncover issues that impeded the therapeutic alliance. So, she stated, "I know that you prefer to have my attending evaluate you. However, I am truly the only person available tonight, and it is not feasible for you to spend the night here in this room. I think it is time for us to explore what your issues are with me and what is keeping you from allowing me to help you. Did I do something to offend you?"

The patient answered, "Well, when I first saw you I thought you looked unprofessional." The resident, shocked by the statement, responded, "Oh, really? What was I wearing that day that made you think my appearance was unprofessional?"

The patient then replied, "It's not that I don't like black people, but..."

The resident inquired, "Have you ever had a black physician?" The patient cynically uttered, "Never, never, never."

Despite the anger and sadness that the resident experienced from hearing these words, she further processed the transference of the patient. "I can now understand why this is so hard for you. But tell me, what does that mean for you to have a black physician?"

Mrs. Goldsmith expressed, "Well, it brings about an issue of competence for me."

Dr. Miller then posed, "Do you think your doctor would have trusted me to be here with you if he didn't feel I was competent?"

"I guess not," replied Mrs. Goldsmith.

Dr. Miller then asked if the patient would allow her to provide a brief initial evaluation and agreed to notify the patient's attending physician of her insistence that Dr. Miller no longer be involved in her treatment.

Later, in her course of treatment, Mrs. Goldsmith sought the help of Dr. Miller. Although difficult for Dr. Miller, maintaining a professional demeanor with the patient served to improve the therapeutic relationship in such a way that the patient sought her assistance throughout the remainder of her hospital stay. This strategy promoted the patient's freedom of expression regarding her racial and ethnic stereotypes.

There are certain instances when a patient offends a doctor that may warrant a change in clinicians. In instances when doctors feel that they cannot regulate their emotions appropriately or feel that their safety is compromised, it would be better to transition the patient's care. As previously mentioned, professionalism also demands that we recognize our own limitations.

When the patient is white and the therapist is black, there is another common scenario. White patients may be particularly prone to deny any reaction to an African American therapist for fear of offending their treater (Leary 2000). They may bend over backward to scotomize any differences between themselves and their psychotherapist.

Mrs. Walters, a middle-aged Caucasian female, was engaged in psycho-therapy for treatment of her depression with Dr. Jones, a young African American trainee therapist. She discussed her experience of hearing de-rogatory comments about African Americans while visiting with friends.

Dr. Jones encouraged further exploration by asking, "What kinds of things were they saying?" She replied, "They know that I like Obama and they continue to say things like he is a Muslim and have nothing positive to say." With tears in her eyes, Mrs. Walters stated, "They can watch blacks play football, but if they are trying to do something good and help others, then they have something negative to say. Dr. Jones, you have to help me figure out what I am going to do." Together the therapist and patient ex-plored ways that she could bring to her friends' attention how she feels when such comments are made. Alternatively, they processed what it would be like for her to not say anything. Dr. Jones then asked her, "What is this like for you, I mean, having this discussion with a black therapist?"

Mrs. Walters paused then stated, "But you're not black. We are sisters in this together. We are the same." Dr. Jones chuckled with a mixture of surprise and embarrassment and replied, "Well, I wonder what your friends would say if they sat in the room with us. I bet they might differ." Mrs. Walters retorted tearfully, "I would say this is the best therapist in the world." Dr. Jones replied, "Mrs. Walters, you do not have to be the spokesperson for me or anyone else. You can speak for yourself here. In fact, whatever views your friends embrace do not negate the work that we do here. I still think we have done some hard work in this therapy, and I think you have accomplished a great deal."

An important aspect of professionalism is recognizing and exploring the ethnic and racial differences and similarities as they influence the clin-ical interaction. In most cases a sense of relief accompanies the anxiety regarding bringing up such matters. The patient may feel recognized and validated. However, as in all clinical work, the timing is crucial. One can introduce a comment about race or ethnic matters when the patient is talking about something else and come across as insensitive or driven by the clinician's own needs rather than the patient's.

Gender and Professionalism

Although there are endless debates about what is truly masculine or truly feminine, there is a growing body of literature suggesting that gender dif-ferences in perception and thinking exist. Women more strongly endorse the importance of ethics and professionalism in medicine than men (Jain et al. 2010; Roberts et al. 2004, 2006). Men place more importance on being objective, whereas women place greater emphasis on preserving relationships (Shapiro and Miller 1994). Men and women approach values-based decisions differently (Price et al. 1998).

Psychiatrists striving for professionalism must recognize that sensitivity to gender in the clinical setting and in the workplace is central. Clinicians tend to make immediate assumptions about patients based on gender. In a manner that is similar to ethnic stereotyping, one may assume qualities based on gender without really exploring the unique features of the patient. Also, there are areas of experience that apply to women from which men are largely excluded—reproduction, menstruation, and so on (Nadelson 1993). Male clinicians need to make a concerted effort to listen and empathize with the emotional phenomena associated with these uniquely feminine features. There is a long historical tradition of male decision making about healthcare policies that affect primarily female patients, such as birth control and abortion.

Initial transferences to clinicians may be profoundly affected by the gender constellation of the therapeutic dyad. Some women may find it hard to open up to a male therapist about childhood sexual abuse at the hands of a male perpetrator. In the transference at the beginning of the treatment, there is a conviction that the therapist has attitudes that are similar to those of the male abuser, and the patient may be deeply worried that an abusive relationship—if only verbal in nature—will develop. Certain issues may only surface with a female therapist. A male patient who was humiliated by his mother may approach a female therapist with trepidation because of an early transference disposition to assume humiliation. If the male patient is struggling with sexual problems, he may choose to conceal them rather than risk humiliation.

An aspect of professionalism is to attune oneself to these preexisting gender considerations and do what one can to pave the way for open exploration of areas that may feel off limits to the patient. Similarly, as in the examples of racial differences cited earlier, one must acknowledge one's limits when it comes to understanding someone who is fundamentally different and welcome the patient's educational efforts to increase his or her understanding. Moreover, there is substantial evidence that some psychiatric illnesses are more frequently found in females, so a good professional must be "gender competent" in the same way that one must be culturally competent.

Sexual Harassment

The setting in which healthcare is delivered is also relevant to this discussion. Although increasing numbers of women are entering the mental health workforce, there continues to be a patriarchal order in many work environments. Women may be more prone to be viewed as sexualized and disempowered. Their perspective is going to be different than that of men because of experiences related to gender stereotypes. Much like the experiences of racial microtraumas discussed earlier, many women have subtle daily experiences of sexism that are a part of the fabric of their daily experience. Professional women may be viewed as less competent than their male counterparts or receive passing sexualized flirtatious comments. Sexual harassment laws rely on definitions of sexual harassment that are based on the "average woman's" view, not how male observers see things. Women have had different experiences of gender-based discrimination and therefore have a different world view than men.

In 1980, the Equal Employment Opportunity Commission specified that sexual harassment is a violation of the 1964 Civil Rights Act under Title VII (Equal Employment Opportunity Commission 1964). It defined *sexual harassment* as unwelcome sexual advances, requests for sexual favors, and other verbal or physical conduct of a sexual nature. In 1986, in *Meritor Savings Bank v. Vinson* (1986), the court distinguished between two types of sexual harassment—*quid pro quo,* where sexual favors are traded for job benefits, and the creation of a hostile work environment. An important component of sexual harassment is that it lacks the elements of choice and mutuality inherent in consenting relationships.

Perhaps the most common situation of sexual harassment involves a man in a position of power harassing a woman who has less authority. For example, a prominent male researcher called the young female graduate students in his department "girl" and "honey" and promised them authorship in return for sexual favors. However, the picture is not always so stereotyped. A male medical student found himself faced with uncomfortable comments from the female attending on his internal medicine rotation. She was a reputable clinician and rising star in her department, and when she started to say things like, "I love how you look when you are presenting the patients to us" and "nice ass" as he walked away from her down the hall, he felt terribly worried. One day she asked him to go for a drink after work, with the implication that his grade would reflect the time he spent with her. He felt uncertain how to proceed, wanting to do well but feeling ashamed and nervous.

The complexity of relationships and power dynamics require that each individual situation be addressed in its particular context. One is hard pressed to make generalizations regarding when sexual harassment is or is not occurring because one must take into account how power is configured in the relationship, the specifics of mutuality in the banter between coworkers, and the way humor is regarded. Context is everything. The perceptions of the person to whom the comments were made must be taken into account. There are certainly situations in which humor is used that are not experienced as threatening or harassing to someone on a treatment team. However, another person in a parallel, but different, context might well feel harassed by similar comments due to the nature of the relationship, the tone of voice, or the perceived implication. It is critical for people working with one another to be sensitive to the potential for harm and misunderstanding.

Erotic Transference and the Management of Boundaries

The cultural issues that define gender relationships broadly as well as individuals' unique histories also may be activated in treatment. Hence the management of professional boundaries and erotic transference may be different for female therapists than for males. Female therapists may actually experience much more of a physical threat to their safety when the patient is a male compared with the situation with a male therapist and female patient. Celenza (2006) made the point that in traditional gender stereotypes in the culture, hardness and the outward direction of aggression are associated with maleness, whereas passivity, softness, and inward direction of aggression are viewed as female. Moreover, men in general tend to be physically stronger than women, which may be the chief difference in sexualized transferences involving a female therapist. The clinical example that follows illustrates these concerns.

> A 27-year-old married male patient saw Dr. Jamison, a female resident, in psychotherapy for 1 year. After several months, he began to ask if they could meet for lunch or if he could have a longer session. Dr. Jamison did not grant these requests but understood with the patient that he felt he had important things to say and time felt short with the therapist. The supervisor helped the therapist clarify the patient's longing for a different kind of relationship while also outlining the boundaries of the therapeutic rela-

tionship. Dr. Jamison also clarified that there would be no meetings outside the office or prolonged sessions. In supervision, they discussed how to share with the patient why boundaries are important to the patient and to the work of therapy.

Early in supervision, the supervisor noted early signs of developing erotic transference. The supervisor and therapist role played how the therapist might respond if the patient developed erotic feelings and attempted to push the boundaries of the therapy. As the therapy proceeded, the patient continued to challenge the frame of the therapy, wondering why he and the therapist could not be friends, particularly after termination. When Dr. Jamison again clarified the boundaries, the patient asserted that the therapist was more rule bound and rigid than compassionate. The supervisor and therapist understood together that the patient experienced his mother as critical and neglectful and thus transferred these qualities to the therapist.

As termination neared, the patient insisted that he knew that the therapist was not married, despite her wedding ring. He confessed his admiration for her beauty and his love for her. He stated he could tell that she loved him as much as he loved her.

The therapist and supervisor collaborated on preparing for the final session, which they both predicted would be challenging. In supervision, they role played different scenarios, such as redirecting physical advances and handling gifts. The supervisor and therapist practiced the management of the therapist's physical proximity to the patient, when to stand up, and how to end the session. The supervisor suggested to the therapist to initiate a handshake rather than waiting to see if the patient would attempt an embrace. They practiced how the therapist could tactfully decline a kiss or hug. They also focused conceptually on a balance between limit setting and inflicting narcissistic injury on the patient. Finally, they anticipated questions about contact after termination, whether by e-mail or phone. The discussion of boundaries with the patient in an ongoing manner is helpful for those who push the limits of the boundaries, because this can be painful and difficult for some patients to understand. The end result was a relatively smooth termination session.

This case allows us to examine the unique features of a particular sexualized transference when the therapist is female and the patient is male. Transferences that are characterized by sexual desire for the therapist reside on a rather extensive spectrum from those involving a shy, deeply conflicted and ashamed male patient on the one hand to a threatening, possibly narcissistic or antisocial male on the other. Female therapists must carefully assess this dimension of risk when undertaking the psychotherapeutic management of such patients (Hobday et al. 2008). Does one explore the meanings of a transference? Or does one set firm limits on what is acceptable in treatment? Moreover, are there instances in which one must end the treatment? A related concern is how much latitude one gives a male patient to explicitly express sexual wishes and fantasies toward the female therapist. At what point do such expressions become verbally abusive and violating in their impact? When does a female therapist feel that she is being devalued and professionally deskilled by being transformed into a sex object? Female therapists facing this dilemma must decide whether their feeling of being demeaned is itself a countertransference problem that they must master or a realistic reaction to outrageous behavior by the patient.

The point at which one sets limits and asks the patient to cease and desist is complicated because one risks conveying that sexual feelings are not acceptable in the therapy or that they can be expressed only in a narrow range within an unspoken set of rules of therapeutic discourse (Gabbard 2005). Especially as a new therapist, these transference behaviors can be exciting, frightening, insulting, or puzzling. The challenge of maintaining a steady therapeutic function while making room for and recognizing countertransference in the face of these behaviors can be substantial. Sexualized transferences often demonstrate an aggressive undercurrent as well (Gabbard 2005). Brenner (1982) suggested that all transferences have multiple layers reflecting both sexuality and aggression. Because it is true that men are generally stronger than women, the safety of the female therapist must be of paramount importance before any therapeutic issues can be considered. The therapist's chair must always be more comfortable than the patient's chair. The previous case example also demonstrates how boundaries must be managed with such patients. We often focus on professional boundaries in the therapist, but the boundary of the psychotherapy also may involve structuring the patient's interaction with the therapist.

One must recognize that there is fluidity in the transference of erotic feelings in the room that are not always dependent on the therapist or the patient's sexual orientation or gender. Erotic transference in patients of the same gender as the therapist can at times bring up unexpected sexualized discussions for which the therapist should be prepared. In addition, patients who are heterosexual can have erotic transference to therapists of the same gender, and those who are homosexual can have sexual and loving feelings to therapists of opposite gender.

Ms. Renshaw, a 41-year-old lesbian woman, entered psychotherapy for her struggles with her romantic relationship and her continual difficulties relating to her male colleagues at work. The patient was seductive and made comments that flattered the therapist, such as "I enjoy watching a woman walk" as she followed her therapist down the hall. When asked about the meaning of these comments, she denied that she was being seductive and said that she knew that the therapist was heterosexual. The therapist had a difficult task in determining whether and when to investigate the behavior or to let it go, as the patient suggested.

Such decisions as the ones facing this therapist are best made with time and knowledge of the specific patient. It is often unclear early on if the patient is unconsciously seductive with people as part of her character or if there is a conscious and deliberate desire to shift the relationship with the therapist to one of two erotic partners on a level playing field. Of course, both of these threads may be present in the tapestry of the psychotherapeutic relationship. It is also true that erotic transferences can remain unspoken for extended periods of time even when the feelings are conscious.

A female patient in her mid-30s attended therapy for 6 months prior to the therapist's initiation of termination without ever behaving in a seductive manner. However, in the last session, the patient professed her love for the therapist and persisted throughout the session in a quest to pursue a romantic relationship following termination. The patient completely lacked the ability to consider in the moment that the psychiatrist was married and likely heterosexual. She also could not describe what she imagined the relationship would look like. She was simply intent on maintaining this important and intimate relationship in her life. For the female therapist, this turn of events was unexpected, and the pressure applied to the therapist to violate professional boundaries was intense.

This scenario exemplifies how important it is for psychiatrists to be well grounded in ethics and boundaries before being exposed to a highly charged emotional experience in the dyad of therapy.

As noted in Chapter 3, in education about therapeutic boundaries it is important to teach that all therapists are vulnerable to boundary violations. As in the example with Dr. Jamison, the patient's attempts to encroach on the therapist's boundaries must be dealt with, whereas in other situations, the therapist's temptations are a greater challenge and must be silently processed by the therapist. Supervision or consultation provides necessary tools and insights regarding management as well as support in challenging situations (Gabbard and Crisp-Han 2010).

Gender, Ethnicity, Culture, and Religion

Although in this chapter we have chosen to take up each of the influences separately, gender, ethnicity, culture, sexual orientation, and religion may all be relevant in one case. In psychotherapy, there are times when gender interfaces with ethnicity, culture, and religion in such a way that the therapist is faced with extraordinary challenges that demand thinking at multiple levels simultaneously.

> Dr. Kadir, a Muslim psychiatric resident of Middle Eastern origin, was seeing a Caucasian female patient of approximately the same age. In the very first session, the patient was struck by the obvious differences between the therapist and herself. She was at first reluctant to bring up the differences. However, she spoke in a halted, formal manner and seemed reluctant to express openly how miserable she was. She spoke of the problems she was having with her domineering husband but did not provide much detail about the conflicts in the marriage. As is often the case, she expressed a covert transference to her therapist in the waning seconds of her session (Gabbard 1982). When she strode to the door, she turned to Dr. Kadir and delivered her exit line, "You're very nice, but I really wonder if you can understand what I'm going through. I can tell from the fact that you cover your hair that you're Muslim, and I know that Muslim women see their husbands as the big authority in the house. I understand that's your religion and all, but I'm worried about that. Do you think you can really help me?" Dr. Kadir astutely avoided trying to deal with a complex concern in a few seconds. Instead, she said, "I'm so glad you could bring up those concerns. Let's both remember to start here when you come next time."
>
> At the beginning of the next session, the patient launched into problems at work, completely avoiding the exchange at the end of the hour. Dr. Kadir waited for an auspicious moment and said, "I can understand that you'd rather not talk about what we ended with last time, but I think it's important to get back to your concerns about whether or not I can understand you." In the ensuing discussion, Dr. Kadir clarified that her own views were actually quite complex (without getting into details about them), and she emphasized to the patient that her role was to appreciate what marriage and gender roles meant to *her.*

As this vignette reflects, it is rarely useful to expound at great length about one's own religious beliefs. Excessive self-disclosure is often experienced by the patient as an unwelcome role reversal. The focus of psychotherapy is on the patient's concerns. Sometimes a simple reassurance that one is capable of appreciating another's perspective with an open mind, followed by a conscientious effort to check out with the patient any unclear communications, is all that is needed to form a solid therapeutic alliance.

Sexual Orientation

Psychiatry has had a complex history regarding sexual orientation. Within the past few decades there have been vast and important changes in how sexuality is viewed in our culture and in psychiatry. There is a long cultural history of the marginalization of people who are gay, lesbian, bisexual, and transgendered as sinful, wrong, or changeable. Given psychiatry's past history of pathologizing people who are homosexual and labeling them as having a specific psychiatric disorder, we must be aware of the historical and cultural currents in the treatment, both consciously and unconsciously, for the clinician and the patient. There may be particular issues that arise in therapy of a person who is coming to therapy for issues regarding sexual orientation. For example, conversations regarding coming out; dealing with homophobia within oneself, the family, or the broader community; issues of identity; empowerment versus shame; and loss of expectations may all emerge in treatment. However, it would be an oversimplification and a disservice to each individual to categorize the psychotherapy only in this manner. Many people are also dealing with depression, anxiety, relationship problems, arguments at work, and other issues that are not specific to their sexuality or gender. Nevertheless, it is important for a therapist to be attuned to the particular developmental struggles that secrecy and marginalization may have led to in the lives of a gay, lesbian, or bisexual patient (Phillips et al. 2005). Respect and empathy for the challenges inherent in living within a homophobic society must be the foundation of the treatment.

One professional issue that clinicians often face when working with gay, lesbian, and bisexual patients involves the emergence of questions regarding the therapist's sexuality. Gay and lesbian therapists then face a dilemma: should they tell the gay patient that they too are gay? Similarly, straight therapists must also decide on the pros and cons of self-disclosure regarding sexual orientation. There are thoughtful therapists who come down on different sides of this controversy—some feel strongly about disclosing, whereas others feel adamantly that such questions should be explored with the patient. Still others find an approach in which they tailor their response to the specifics of the case. An affirmative answer by a gay therapist might lead to a sense of kinship and mutual understanding for a patient who has been immersed in a world of shame and secrecy. However, it might also lead to idealization and false assumptions about similarities between the therapist's views and the patient's views. Sometimes there are many questions behind the question of the therapist's sexual orientation: Are you like me or not? Will you understand my experience? Can you help me? Can you introduce me to your friends? Are you someone who has made it through this difficult experience? Will I be okay like you? As the therapist is deciding how and whether to answer, it is usually helpful to find out what is behind the wish to know the psychiatrist's sexual orientation.

Just as clinicians may want to consider the situation regarding whether to reveal their sexual orientation, the issue of neutrality in the therapy also arises. Often, questions of sexuality are present in people who are not at all sure of where they stand, and there is a risk of the therapist's making facile assumptions regarding whether the patient is gay, straight, or bisexual. As we understand sexuality further, we realize that although there are probably genetic underpinnings to sexual orientation, there is also considerable fluidity in desire throughout the life cycle. The complexity of how individuals come to understand themselves and the fact that it may unfold over time must be respected. One can have multiple sexual fantasies, experiences, and thoughts without defining oneself in a particular manner. For example, a woman may come to a psychiatrist and say, "I had sex with another woman, but I have always been attracted to men. We are close friends, and I love her, and now I am not sure."

It would be presumptive and certainly too early in the process for the clinician to tell her that she must be a lesbian, or bisexual, or that she must make a decision. It is far more helpful and professional to be curious about her feelings, her experiences, and her childhood background and to try to help her understand herself and what is going on internally. Moreover, just as we all may have unconscious prejudices regarding race because of growing up in the society in which we live, we may also have unconscious homophobic tendencies that influence how we think about our patients. Because sexuality is not a psychiatric diagnosis, it may be more fruitful to think of oneself as on a shared journey to help people discover sexual desire and orientation for themselves rather than proclaiming it from above. Developmental crises, such as those involving the transition from adolescence to young adulthood or midlife, may include careful considerations of identity and desire that will settle out only with time and reflection.

An important component of professionalism is avoiding the position that psychiatrists can and should change sexual orientation. There are some therapists who promote a type of therapy called *conversion therapy*, in which they claim that they are able to change the sexual orientation of a homosexual person. Phillips et al. (2005) have charted the long history of bias against different sexualities, the tendency to view variations as pathology, and the more recent push toward gay-affirmative therapy as a psychiatric stance in treatment. The mainstream trend to recognize sexual orientation as unlikely to change with psychotherapy led to a counter-movement toward conversion or reparative therapy, in which the treatment is aimed at changing sexual orientation. Finally, there has been a counter-shift back toward a neutral position, allowing each person to explore his or her sexuality, with the emphasis on the need for the patient to discover an authentic sense of self (Phillips et al. 2005).

Drescher (1998) traced a detailed history of the reparative therapy movement. In a 2000 position statement on therapies focused on changing sexual orientation (reparative or conversion therapies), the American Psychiatric Association (APA) affirmed its 1973 position that homosexuality is not a diagnosable mental disorder and opposed any psychiatric treatment that is based on the assumption that homosexuality is a disorder: "Recent publicized efforts to re-pathologize homosexuality by claiming it can be cured are often guided not by rigorous scientific or psychiatric research, but sometimes by religious and political forces opposed to full civil rights for gay men and lesbians" (American Psychiatric Association 2000). The APA recognized that the discussion of reparative therapies is located in a political context in the culture. They noted that the success rates cited in the literature are based upon "anecdotal" reports of individuals, in which the reports of "cure" are balanced with reports of harm. The social stigma of homosexuality is not addressed in motivating efforts to change sexual orientation, and the literature tends to overstate the accomplishments of the treatment while neglecting any potential risks to patients.

Until further research is available, the APA recommends that ethical practitioners refrain from attempts to change sexual orientation. The APA is not alone in its position—in its criticism of or opposition to reparative therapies it joins other professional organizations, such as the American Medical Association, the American Psychological Association, the American Counseling Association, and the National Association of Social Workers.

This position is not only a subject of cultural, religious, or political debate but also an issue that strikes at the heart of one's work as a psychiatrist or other mental health professional. In medicine, there are ethical duties to adhere to beneficence and nonmalfeasance. Regarding professionalism, one must rely on the literature and collegial consensus to determine best practices. While looking externally to research, we must also look inside ourselves to our own inevitable prejudgments, affiliations, and countertransferences. Thoroughgoing neutrality is rarely possible, because all of us come into the consulting room with our own histories and unconscious biases. It is necessary to look at our patients and ourselves and be continuously curious about discovering our own biases and prejudices (Mitchell 1996) and work through those in ourselves as clinicians.

When the psychiatrist or therapist is gay or lesbian, there can be subtle issues that arise in a practice situation, much like themes involving gender or ethnicity. How does a gay psychiatrist deal with it when a patient is angrily homophobic and goes on rants that are demeaning without consciously knowing that his physician is gay? How the psychiatrist handles this situation could be different if it were in an outpatient therapeutic setting versus an inpatient setting versus a one-time emergency department contact. The response could also differ depending on the level of the patient's functioning, although the psychiatrist's internal feelings might be similar. Supervision or consultation is important to manage hurt or angry countertransference feelings, particularly with ongoing relationships, and to ensure that a problematic enactment does not occur. What if the demeaning person is not a patient but a colleague within the work setting? What does a gay or lesbian psychiatrist do about a professional colleague who decides not to refer patients once he learns of the psychiatrist's sexual orientation? We all like to believe we are in a culture in which these issues are improving and prejudice is diminishing. However, the discrimination against people who are gay, lesbian, and bisexual continues to exist in both subtle and overt ways. Open, kind, and respectful communication with colleagues—heterosexual or homosexual—can pave the way for discussing misunderstandings, and certainly questions of discrimination and harassment should be addressed as such. One central tenet of professionalism is to consider people as individuals, rather than stereotypes, and to avoid the stigmatizing use of labeling.

Key Points

- Psychiatrists should strive for cultural empathy, in which they immerse themselves in the patient's experience of the world.

- Unconscious prejudice is ubiquitous and must be taken into account in both clinician and patient.

- A legacy of racism may lead black patients to develop negative institutional transferences toward the healthcare system.

- Racial differences between patient and therapist are often avoided by both parties.

- Erroneous assumptions about the other party in the therapist-patient dyad are common when race/ethnicity are similar.

- Women may experience microtraumas of gender in the same way African Americans experience racial microtraumas.

- Female therapists must place safety as a high priority as they assess whether it makes sense to explore the meanings of a male patient's erotic transference.

- Fluidity of desire and gender identification is common in psychotherapy.

- Excessive self-disclosure of the therapist's belief system is rarely productive, but inquiry about the patient's cultural and religious values may build cultural empathy and sensitivity.

- It is not professional or ethical to attempt to change a patient's sexual orientation.

- Therapists must often tolerate extended periods of uncertainty as patients explore who they are and what they desire.

Chapter 7

Overlapping Roles and Conflicts of Interest

A difficult ethical tension exists for all professionals: professionals are expected to use their expertise through diverse and multiple roles to bring benefit to others in society, yet these very same roles may introduce potential conflicts of interest. For this reason, overlapping roles are natural and predictable for professionals, and they are not inherently unethical. In fact, some would argue that a physician who does not also serve as a teacher, scientist, administrator, consultant, or community leader is failing to give fully to the society that has entrusted him with performing work of value to others. This said, overlapping roles fulfilled by professionals *always and without exception* introduce new ethical challenges and risks.

Sometimes the ethical risk inherent in overlapping roles is obvious: for instance, physicians certainly may be tempted by clear opportunities for personal financial gain. One example would be the psychiatrist who works in a healthcare system that incentivizes short lengths of stay and the use of inexpensive medications but does not evaluate quality of care in their metrics. In this situation, the financial rewards for the physician and the well-being of the patient may diverge completely. Although the physician is, of course, obligated to provide compassionate and competent care, this commitment is tested continuously in this circumstance. The potential for self-interested bias shaping clinical decisions is essentially "institutionalized" and represents a substantial "threat" to the integrity of the physician.

President Barack Obama highlighted the issue of misaligned and distorted incentives in his speech to the American Medical Association shortly after assuming the executive office ("Obama Addresses Physicians at AMA Meeting" 2009). He said,

> Today we are spending over $2 trillion a year on health care—almost 50% more per person than the next most costly nation. And yet, for all this spending, more of our citizens are uninsured; the quality of our care is often lower; and we aren't any healthier....Make no mistake: the cost of our health care is a threat to our economy....What accounts for the bulk of our costs is the nature of our health care system itself—a system where we spend vast amounts of money on things that aren't making our people any healthier; a system that automatically equates more expensive care with better care....There are two main reasons for this. The first is a system of incentives where the more tests and services are provided, the more money we pay. And a lot of people in this room know what I'm talking about. It is a model that rewards the quantity of care rather than the quality of care; that pushes you, the doctor, to see more and more patients even if you can't spend much time with each; and gives you every incentive to order that extra MRI or EKG, even if it's not truly necessary.

President Obama directly commented on the fundamental threat to professionalism that this incentivized approach represents. He remarked that physicians had been reduced to "accountants" and concluded that this "is a model that has taken the pursuit of medicine from a profession—a calling—to a business."

These comments corresponded with a number of concerns outlined in a substantial report of the Institute of Medicine, released at nearly the same time as this speech, and resonated with key points of documents by the Association of American Medical Colleges and others. Individual and institutional conflicts of interest were the focus of much of this national discussion, with the greatest debate developing around conflicts of interest in human research. Of greatest ethical concern were industry-supported clinical trials bringing new medications and devices to the field of medicine. This attention is not surprising, because funding for industry-sponsored research had increased explosively, with estimated expenditures rising from $1.5 billion in 1980 to $22 billion two decades later, with $6 billion designated for clinical trials alone in 2001 (Warner and Gluck 2003; Warner and

Roberts 2004). This overall emphasis on investment by industry in research was far, far greater (i.e., 1,367% increase between 1980 and 2001) than increases experienced by the National Institutes of Health (209% increase from 1985 to 1999, up to $13.9 billion) or the National Science Foundation (150% increase up to $3.5 billion in 2001).

Psychiatrists who are also researchers do, in fact, experience many pressures related to their overlapping roles. Financial conflicts of interest are commonplace. It is often rumored, for instance, that psychiatrist-investigators may "soften" eligibility criteria so that they may enroll patients in clinical trials, thereby garnering recruitment "bonuses" and gaining favor with the company sponsor. Similarly, psychiatrist-investigators may minimize or ignore protocol patients' distress in order to keep the subjects enrolled in the trial, thereby receiving additional compensation and retention "bonuses," often amounting to many thousands of dollars. Psychiatrist-investigators who engage in such activity thus fail to fulfill their professional duties as psychiatrists by not honoring their commitments to patients to be respectful, beneficent, and fair in their interactions. They also fail to fulfill their professional duties as researchers, however, by not being honest and not performing rigorous scientific work that will bring forward data of value to society.

Consider a second example in which the ethical risks related to personal gain for a psychiatric researcher are more indirect but still very potent. An academic psychiatrist performs a study supported by the National Institutes of Health, and the study focuses on the effectiveness of an old "off-patent" medication and a new medication that has been introduced to the marketplace recently. The new medication is made by a company for which the academic psychiatrist serves as a consultant and "opinion leader," receiving payment of up to $50,000 each year above his medical school salary. The investigator may be tempted to design trials that enhance the likelihood of finding results in support of strong performance by the new medication or, alternatively, he may be tempted to slow down—or even suppress—the reporting of data regarding the discovery of weak performance or serious side effects associated with the new medication.

In a meta-analysis study by Warner and Gluck in 2003, it was found that one-fifth of investigators in published surveys on research integrity issues acknowledged that they had delayed publication of data for more than 6 months during the prior 3 years in order to safeguard personal interests or to avoid disclosure of unfavorable outcomes, and this was more likely if the researcher had a financial relationship with industry. That so many practice guidelines are constructed by professionals with ties to industry is also a concern that has increased over the past decade.

In a scathing critique of American medicine, *The Lancet* highlighted the finding in a *JAMA* report documenting that almost 90% of authors of practice guidelines in 2002 had received industry funding ("Just How Tainted Has Medicine Become?" 2002). President Obama also more gently alluded to this issue on how guidelines "without evidence" exist in this country for many serious diseases. Whether or not an investigator's actions are intentional or constitute actual misconduct, the situation of two overlapping roles does produce pressures that may influence, and perhaps negatively distort, the judgment of the professional, as these data suggest. *The Lancet* editors were critical of their own colleagues' interests and questioned whether editorial decisions were free from bias:

> [T]he editor of the *British Journal of Psychiatry* was recently questioned about his membership in a drug-company sponsored "educational organization," for which he received £2000 annually, together with his decision to publish a paper favouring a drug manufactured by the same company. Only after receiving the letter questioning his behaviour did the editor change his journal's procedure, excluding himself from decisions about work sponsored by that same company. He avoided the issue about whether he should have any commercial liaisons while acting as editor of a supposedly independent medical journal. (p. 1167)

The field of psychiatry does itself no favors when issues of this sort arise.

More subtle conflicts of interest come with other overlapping roles that are poorly aligned and the responsibilities or "interests" of one role compete for, or are "trumped" by, the interests of a second role. Personal financial gain may be an element in such situations, but other ethical considerations may also arise. Before turning to illustrations prevalent in the popular press related to physician-industry relationships, in order to understand the ethics issues uncomplicated by financial incentive considerations it is instructive to look at other kinds of dual roles.

Let us turn first to the phenomenon of informal care or "curbside consultation," in which a physician provides care for a friend, colleague, supervisor, or family member. Curbside consultation occurs frequently. An early study by La Puma et al. (1991), for instance, revealed that 99% of 465 physicians in a large suburban hospital had been approached by family members for informal care, and 83% had prescribed medications, 80% had diagnosed medical illnesses, 72% had performed physical examinations,

15% served as the primary caregivers for a family member, and 9% had performed surgery on a family member. In a later study, 41% of medical students ($n=112$) in a pilot project had informally consulted with a resident or attending to obtain healthcare (Roberts et al. 1996), and in a nine-site follow-up study, 63% of 1,027 medical students used informal care (Roberts et al. 2001).

In these "curbside consultation" situations, the clinician serves in a dual role as caregiver *and* friend, colleague, supervisor, or family member, and the patient serves in a dual role as care-seeker *and* friend, colleague, supervisor, or family member. The care-seeker's motives for this "curbside" consultative arrangement might be straightforward, for example, an exhausted medical student sub-intern with known strep exposure and a sore throat who requests antibiotics from his resident, or a family member with no health insurance who requests medical advice and a renewal of a long-standing prescription. The caregiver's motivation, although not related to financial interest, might be as simple as wanting to be helpful, but the result is that the care-seeker will be "beholden" to the "dual-role clinician." Furthermore, the dual-role clinician now has information that may affect the life of the "dual-role patient" in unexpected ways, for example, the attending physician who sits on the student progress and evaluation committee who knows perhaps a "little too much" about the student's personal health issues. Finally, the care provided under such circumstances is not accountable in the manner that all other healthcare is. This creates ethical risk, because usual practices (e.g., chart review, thoroughness, follow-up care) that assure clinical competence and transparency are not followed.

The potential for vulnerability inherent in dual roles is reflected in the attitudes expressed by workers, residents, and medical students regarding the use, or misuse, of their personal health information in the employment or training setting. A study of 1,027 medical students at nine sites revealed that 90% indicated a need for personal healthcare, 90% stated that they preferred to obtain care away from their training institution, and 70% said that this choice was based on confidentiality concerns. The greatest desire for off-site care was correlated with stigmatizing conditions that were perceived as producing academic "jeopardy" based on prejudice rather than actual academic performance. These studies help to show how even well-intended actions by individuals in overlapping roles may be seen as creating vulnerability or jeopardy and may actually or appear to produce harm (Roberts et al. 2001).

In the absence of adequate safeguards, similar concerns also arise despite the positive hopes and constructive goals of overlapping roles in clinical and industry partnerships.

> The director of a clinic for underserved and seriously mentally ill patients in an academic setting speaks routinely with representatives from several different pharmaceutical companies who are rigorously compliant with medical school policies regarding interactions with "industry." Together the clinic director and the representatives work closely to develop proactive "Patient Assistance Program" contracts between the medical school and the companies to help provide medications for eligible disadvantaged patients in the clinic. Over time, some of the company representatives transition away from the area, and eventually only two continue the collaborative effort with the clinic director. Because of many difficult economic issues, patients in the clinic increasingly are prescribed only the six medications for which assistance program support is available.

This is a scenario in which the clinic director does not receive any personal financial benefit through the relationship with the pharmaceutical companies, and it is clear that many patients in the clinic had greater access to care, in the form of medication treatment, by virtue of the academic–industry collaboration. Nevertheless, the ethical risks become clear as the implicit "safeguard" in the situation—that is, working with multiple companies that provide a diverse array of medication options—is lost. The clinic, the clinic's patients, and the clinic's director may become increasingly reliant on just a few representatives to provide medications, and this produces a situation in which appropriate standards of care may be eroded and the clinic becomes more beholden to fewer and increasingly empowered "partners."

Gift-giving is always ethically complex in psychiatry, and this has, at its root, the ethical commitments of the psychiatrist-therapist who is obligated not to exploit the potential vulnerability of the patient entrusted to his care (see Chapter 3). Philanthropic gifts are no less of an ethical challenge for psychiatric-administrators than the gift of jewelry or a watch would be to a psychiatrist-clinician.

> Dr. Matthews served as the chairman of psychiatry in a community-based hospital system and was approached by one of her patients regarding a possible donation to create a new hospital program for people with affective disorders. The patient had remained in treatment for many years but had been, in Dr. Matthews's mind, one of her more "difficult cases."

The patient was extremely wealthy, and he was known as an important leader and benefactor in the area. The gift was quite large by usual standards at the hospital.

Dr. Matthews felt she was in a real bind. There was a "grateful patient" policy that permits caregivers to solicit and receive such gifts, but she knew that the American Psychiatric Association prohibited accepting gifts from patients. Still, Dr. Matthews confided to a supervisor, "I am not sure how that rule works when you are a hospital leader, not just a treating psychiatrist." She would like to accept the gift, because it would bring much good to the hospital and the neighboring community. She was already hearing rumors about the patient's expected largesse, and she received a call of congratulations from a member of the hospital board. Over the course of the patient's care, she had learned much about the patient's financial situation and knew that the patient could afford the size of the gift proffered without hardship.

On the other hand, her instincts told her that "this is all wrong!" She had been the treater for this patient for many years and knew that at least part of his motivation was to "prove" himself as "worthy" and as important to her—this was a central theme that had come up repeatedly over the course of his treatment. It had come up more often since she returned from maternity leave after the birth of her first child 6 months earlier and in recent weeks after the patient learned that his brother had been diagnosed with testicular cancer.

Dr. Matthews spoke with her supervisor about the matter on a few occasions, and then she spoke with an ethics consultant at a national ethics center. She decided to raise several issues and concerns with the patient before informing him that she could not accept the gift. When she approached the question of what prompted the desire to make a donation to the hospital, the patient initially became embarrassed, then tearful, then angry. He told her, "I guess I have to get cancer like my brother before I will get anyone to take me seriously around here. Or maybe you just need another million bucks!"

The care of this patient vividly illustrates how Dr. Matthews's roles as caregiver-psychiatrist and as a department chair–hospital leader have very different obligations. The clinician's obligation is to serve the well-being and best interests of the patient; the department chair/hospital leader's obligation is sound stewardship of excellent clinical programs. Under most circumstances, these obligations may be very tightly aligned; in this circumstance, the obligations of the clinician must prevail so that the patient's vulnerability is not exploited by the system for inappropriate financial gain. As we discussed in Chapter 3, it is clear that the desire to give the gift is affected and perhaps governed wholly by psychopathology. The patient's expression of intent to make the donation was, in fact, a sign of significant clinical distress. The origin of the distress was multifactorial, and it would require very careful intervention. Dr. Matthews was, in fact, in a "bind" because of the dual role she had, but her "instincts" were correct and she was wise to focus on the care of her patient, sidestepping the issue of a philanthropic gift.

Gifts from industry to practicing physicians are, as a recent Institute of Medicine (2009) report indicated, "ubiquitous." Many complain that receiving "a pen or a sandwich from a drug rep" is not going to change their decision making as clinicians, and yet the practice of gift giving with clinicians opens the profession of medicine to the criticism of being untrustworthy and placing personal interests above those of patients.

Physicians and researchers must exercise judgment in complex situations that are fraught with uncertainty. Colleagues, patients, students, and the public need to trust that these judgments are not compromised by physicians' or researchers' financial ties to pharmaceutical, medical device, and biotechnology companies. Ties with industry are common in medicine. Some have produced important benefits, particularly through research collaborations that improve individual and public health. At the same time, widespread relationships with industry have created significant risks that individual and institutional financial interests may unduly influence professionals' judgments about the primary interests or goals of medicine. Such conflicts of interest threaten the integrity of scientific investigations, the objectivity of medical education, and the quality of patient care. They may also jeopardize public trust in medicine.

Whether conflicts of interest truly affect judgments of conscientious clinicians is an empirical question. Nevertheless, it is abundantly clear that the public trust in medicine has indeed been compromised by the close, poorly rationalized, and poorly communicated connections that exist between medicine and industry.

The reliance on industry sources to fulfill "core educational missions" of medical schools and teaching hospitals was identified as a serious concern of the Association of American Medical Colleges in 2008. Continuing medical education, in particular, is heavily dependent on industry support, and this has emerged as a key example of a conflict of interest that may, as noted in the Institute of Medicine report, introduce bias and diminish objectivity in educational efforts. A large meta-analysis of 29 studies (Wazana 2000) revealed that physicians' attitudes toward medications and their prescribing practices were directly influenced by interactions with industry (pharmaceutical) representatives, including attending continuing medical education conferences sponsored by these companies. To minimize the negative effects of these interactions, the American Association of Medical Colleges has encouraged continuing medical education programs to obtain accreditation through an academically based oversight office. This process is intended to assure educational quality and content and to minimize and eliminate scientific bias that may be introduced by the sponsors of research.

A very common scenario helps to illustrate the professionalism issues raised in this national-level discussion.

> A psychiatrist in rural private practice participated in a continuing education dinner event entitled "Modern Approaches to the Care of Depression." The dinner was held at a very posh restaurant, and he received a check for $150 for his participation. The speaker was a prominent subspecialist and held a position at an academic center in a neighboring state. The speaker used slides prepared by the pharmaceutical company hosting the event, and at no time during the talk did the speaker mention recent evidence regarding cognitive-behavioral, interpersonal, or dynamic therapies and their value, with and without medications, in the care of depression.

In this scenario, the main ethical issue pertains to scientific bias and the distortions in clinical practice that may result from a presentation by a subspecialist with academic credentials that purports to cover "modern approaches" and yet does not encompass psychological interventions with demonstrated effectiveness and efficacy in the care of mood disorders. The use of slides provided by the pharmaceutical company creates the impression that treatment recommendations will favor the prescription of medications rather than provision of combined or alternative therapies. These biases and distortions therefore may influence patient care and drive it in the direction of profit for the sponsor of the educational program, whereas a more balanced educational presentation would not necessarily do so.

A second ethical issue inherent in this scenario relates to influences and perhaps coercive pressures experienced by the physician-participants. Enjoying a fancy dinner and receiving an additional check of $150, taken together, may create a significant pressure to attend the event. A further ethical issue relates to the special issues that arise in rural settings, where professionals often have extended roles and become exhausted because of the shortages of care providers, whether primary care or specialty practitioners. Few opportunities exist for additional professional training in rural settings as well. This means that additional pressures may be experienced by rural caregivers who are relatively isolated and more eager (or, therefore, potentially more exploitable) in light of their need for additional educational venues and an expanded skill set necessary for their work.

In summary, overlapping roles are usual, not exceptional, in the lives of physicians. Overlapping roles always and without exception give rise to ethical tensions, and they require careful monitoring and mastering. This is why individually felt and individually enacted professionalism is so critical to public trust in the field of medicine. For psychiatrists, we serve in so many different roles, have so many different subspecialty areas, and engage in so many different activities, and our patients are oftentimes so marginalized, so stigmatized, and so disadvantaged that their vulnerability heightens the potential ethical concerns we can encounter. Furthermore, conflicts of interest may occur on individual as well as organizational levels. For these reasons, extra attention to these professionalism issues is warranted in our field; the potential for ethical risk and the wide variation in the kinds of role tensions, and therefore of ethical problems, are substantial. In the section that follows we offer several strategies for identifying and managing conflicts that naturally occur in the work of a psychiatrist.

Identifying and Managing Conflicts of Interest

Being able to identify ethical considerations is the first ethics skill necessary for the professional (Chapter 2). Recognizing a potential conflict associated with overlapping roles and misaligned duties is fundamental. The Institute of Medicine (2009) report formally defined a *conflict of interest* as "a set of circumstances that creates a risk that professional judgment or actions regarding a primary interest will be unduly influenced by a secondary influence" (p. 25). In this context, a primary interest of the profession of medicine would include "promoting and protecting the integrity of research, the welfare of patients, and the quality of medical education" whereas a secondary interest would include personal financial benefit, the "desire for professional advancement," favored status or standing among others, and the like. It is important to note that these secondary interests are not unethical; they are societally acceptable, but they should not outweigh primary interests.

John Gregory described this exact tension in the 1700s, when he talked about how physician service should not be governed by financial reward but by the virtue of self-sacrifice. Coverdale et al. (2009) summarized Gregory's position as more moderate than it appears at first: "if physicians commit themselves to scientific and ethical excellence in the practice of medicine" they will be successful and "in the long run, the market will recognize and reward" (p. 419) these efforts.

Similarly, the Institute of Medicine further clarified that conflicts should not be viewed in an "all or nothing," black-and-white way: they should be viewed on a graduated scale of seriousness. In addition, the responses and consequences defined in organizational and national policies should demonstrate four qualities—proportionality, transparency, accountability, and fairness—to be appropriate in working constructively with conflicts of interest.

Beyond identifying a conflict, the likelihood of undue influence and the potential for harm should be evaluated. Does the secondary interest, for example, financial gain or professional advancement, jeopardize a primary interest such as patient well-being or educational integrity? Once these concerns have been thought through and sorted out, there are two "next questions" to be considered. First, is additional information needed to determine the true risk in the situation? If so, the individual should seek evidence, expertise, and counsel from appropriate sources to more fully evaluate the concerns. Second, does the gravity of the situation suggest that additional safeguard measures be put in place?

Safeguards and special protections surrounding conflict of interest are many in number, as shown in Table 7–1.

Role separation, when possible, is the most robust safeguard. This may involve withdrawal from one or both of the roles or recusal from participation in key decisions or discussions relevant to a possible role conflict. A second method is full disclosure to all relevant stakeholders in the situation, with special efforts to assure that the potential conflict is understood by those most likely to be endangered or otherwise harmed by the situation. These disclosures should be evaluated carefully in light of their seriousness. The evaluation should be performed with someone at "arm's length" distance and therefore greater objectivity in the situation to whatever extent possible.

TABLE 7–1.   **Principal methods for safeguarding primary**
interests when role conflicts exist

Role separation

Disclosure

Limit setting

Diversification

Information and education

Ongoing monitoring and oversight

Consequences for policy nonadherence

Efforts to limit the parameters affecting the potential for undue influence represent the third safeguard approach. One example of this method is an institution placing limits on funds that researchers can receive or curtailing nonessential travel associated with trials. Diversification of sources to minimize the risk of overdependence on one relationship is another strategy used in reducing conflicts of interest. Ongoing monitoring of key decisions that may be colored by the overlapping role and their inherent interests is another safeguard method. This may be performed by an individual or a committee, properly constituted, and this oversight group must have sufficient authority to verify adherence to a "protected" approach to the situation. The group should be empowered to discontinue some aspect of the situation, if necessary, in order to interrupt potentially or actually dangerous situations that may arise related to the role conflict. Through these efforts, the role conflict may be eliminated or minimized. In addition, active efforts to remain informed and well educated (i.e., information and education) about conflict of interest issues that may arise in unique or not-so-unique situations of medicine, "best practices" at other institutions, and model policies are very important and can do much to assure the minimization of conflict of interest problems.

Beyond these steps, organizations will need policies (and therefore professionals should be aware of the provisions of these policies) that assure an appropriate intervention if the conflict of interest management plan is not followed. Nonadherence to policies should have clear consequences. These steps might include "formative" educational feedback for nonadherence in lower-risk, lower-harm situations, but they will also likely include penalties in higher-risk, higher-harm situations.

So how might these methods to address and minimize the ethical tensions in overlapping relationships operate in the real work of psychiatrists? For instance, recall the earlier case example of the academic clinic director who works with industry sponsors to foster access to patient assistance program medications for the clinic's patients. The director's efforts to continue to diversify the industry relationships so that the clinic does not become overly dependent on certain medications from a single source, or few sources, are very important. It is also critical that she disclose the current programmatic arrangements with her clinic staff, residents, and attending physicians and develop proactive ways to assure that patients receive an appropriate quality of care in the clinic. The academic organization should have carefully built contracts with the industry sponsors so that there is transparency and centralized monitoring of the medication program. It should be clear that the director should not receive any personal financial benefit from these arrangements, and the oversight of the clinic should incorporate potential conflict of interest review. This management strategy thus involves diversification, disclosure, education, monitoring and oversight, limits, and policy adherence.

In 2008, Darrell Kirch, President of the Association of American Medical Colleges, asked, "What will it take to fully affirm our integrity in the public eye?" He stated that we as a profession have been "reluctant to confront" this hard issue and expressed, with chagrin, the fact that despite progress in our attitudes, "we continue to be besieged by headlines and negative public reaction about...embarrassing entanglements with industry" (p. 3). It appears we are at the crossroads. By honestly recognizing overlapping relationships and addressing the resultant potential conflicts and tensions that arise, we have an opportunity to make the "walk" of our profession line up with the "talk" of our profession.

Key Points

- **Overlapping roles are natural and predictable for professionals and are not inherently unethical, but they always give rise to ethical tensions that require careful monitoring.**

- **A *conflict of interest* is defined as "a set of circumstances that creates a risk that professional judgment or actions regarding a** primary interest will be unduly influenced by a secondary influence."

- Being able to identify ethical considerations is the first ethics skill necessary for the professional.

- Psychiatrists commonly encounter financial conflicts of interest.

- Psychiatrists who are researchers experience many pressures related to their overlapping roles. Interaction with industry-supported research and clinical trials is an area of special concern. The psychiatrist-researcher must be aware that the situation of two overlapping roles does produce pressures that may influence, and perhaps negatively distort, the judgment of the professional.

- A nonfinancial example of a dual-role is the "curbside consultation" in which a physician provides care for a friend, colleague, supervisor, or family member. The care provided under such circumstances is not accountable in the manner that all other healthcare is. This fact creates ethical risk, because usual practices that assure clinical competence and transparency are not followed.

- Even well-intended actions by individuals in overlapping roles may be seen as creating vulnerability or jeopardy and may actually or appear to produce harm.

- Gift-giving is always ethically complex in psychiatry, and this practice has, at its root, the ethical commitments of the psychiatrist-therapist who is obligated to avoid exploitation of the potential vulnerability of the patient entrusted to his or her care. Philanthropic gifts are no less of an ethical challenge for psychiatric-administrators than the gift of jewelry or a watch would be to a psychiatrist-clinician.

- Policies addressed at managing conflicts of interests at the organizational and national level should include the qualities of *proportionality, transparency, accountability,* and *fairness* to work constructively with conflicts of interest.

- Special protections and safeguards to manage the inevitable exposure to conflicts of interest include role separation, full disclosure, setting up parameters that limit the potential for undue influence, diversification, ongoing monitoring of overlapping roles, oversight groups with sufficient authority, active efforts to remain informed and well-educated regarding conflict of interest issues, and clear consequences for those who choose not to follow policies.

Chapter 8

Interprofessional and Intercollegial Relationships

In December 2008, *The New York Times* (Tarkan 2008) ran an article in the "Science Times" section entitled "Arrogant, Abusive, and Disruptive—and a Doctor." The article described how physicians behaving badly are increasingly responsible for low morale, high turnover, and stress among professional colleagues, administrative staff, and others with whom they work. The report recounted instances of doctors who erupted in rage at nurses, and the author made a link between disruptive behavior and medical mistakes. The reporter also cited a survey finding that 40% of hospital staff members had reported being so intimidated by a physician that they did not share their concerns about medication orders that appeared to be incorrect. The Joint Commission (2008) is requiring hospitals to have a written code of conduct to prevent this kind of disruptive behavior. Allied health professionals and other healthcare workers have resigned because of experiences of being belittled, insulted, or intimidated by physicians in the workplace.

Shouting at clinical personnel and administrative staff, with public humiliation and temper outbursts, has been part of the negative culture of medicine and medical training from time immemorial. Some of the great surgeons were legendary for their perfectionism in the operating room, manifested in violent temper tantrums when things did not go as they expected. Instruments were thrown, operating room technicians were shoved, and medical students and residents holding retractors had their knuckles rapped with forceps. These role models were internalized as "acceptable" during one's clinical training, and many impressionable young physicians may even have felt a kind of awe at the bravado demonstrated by these senior colleagues. The everyday life of medicine was filled with the doctors who could "get away with anything," especially if they were bright and aggressive in their clinical work. Early career physicians learned that such behavior had to be tolerated from certain "prima donnas" (who were not exclusively in surgical subspecialties). There was an air of resignation with this realization, largely prompted by an acceptance that there was not much you could do it about it except put up with it and hope that you would not fall victim to the next tantrum or attack.

Attitudes have changed, as times have changed. Just as sexual harassment is no longer tolerated in the workplace, bullying, humiliation, and intimidation through anger are increasingly governed by zero tolerance policies in most hospitals and other healthcare organizations. Indeed, the rise of professionalism as a core component of medical education was prompted by such egregious breeches of interprofessional relatedness. Physicians now routinely lose their medical staff privileges, are reported to licensing boards, and are brought before peer review committees when such behaviors become habitual.

Nevertheless, the culture of medicine appears to be at a crossroads: the field of medicine aspires to professionalism, with healthy and constructive role models demonstrating respect, supportive and responsive leadership, and concern for the well-being of patients as well as their colleagues who are responsible for the care of the patients who will be in their care the next day and the day after. Yet it is clear that the disruptive physician is an enduring concern in clinical and training settings, and there are uncertain— but certainly adverse—consequences for both patients and multidisciplinary colleagues and trainees when the culture of medicine is damaged by the presence of negative, influential clinicians who do not uphold and fulfill professionalism ideals.

The Disruptive Physician

Much of the disturbing conduct of doctors has been subsumed under the frequently used rubric of "disruptive physician" in the discourse of the contemporary culture of medicine (Myers and Gabbard 2008). The American Medical Association (2001), in its Code of Medical Ethics, offers the following definition of this term: "personal conduct, whether verbal or physical, that negatively affects or that potentially may negatively affect patient care constitutes disruptive behavior." Prevailing attitudes regarding the importance of professionalism in medicine suggest that disruptive conduct is not common. The truth may be sadly disappointing.

Evidence from diverse sources indicates that disruptive physician behavior is prevalent even in the current environment of medicine. For example, in a 2004 study Weber found that 96% of more than 1,600 physician executives routinely encountered disruptive behavior of physician colleagues, including disrespect, refusal to perform duties appropriately, yelling, and threatening physical behavior. The majority indicated that disruptive behavior is underreported, in part because of the fear of reprisal or retribution in the work environment. Moreover, nurses were most commonly the recipients of inappropriate physician behavior in this study. Similarly, a study published in 2005 revealed that the vast majority (86%) of 675 nurses surveyed had recently witnessed disruptive physician behavior (Rosenstein and O'Daniel 2005).

A survey of physicians, nurses, healthcare executives, and other health workers (Rosenstein and O'Daniel 2008) revealed that 77% had witnessed disruptive behavior in physicians. Sixty-seven percent of the respondents agreed that disruptive behaviors were linked to adverse events, such as medical errors and patient mortality.

If it is the case that learners tend to identify with their teachers, and if some of these teachers are indeed "aggressors" with respect to bullying behavior, we may have some insight as to the origins of these disruptive behaviors. Each year all of the physicians who have completed 1 year of residency training are approached by the Association of American Medical Colleges to comment on their experiences during medical school. The most recently published results (American Association of Medical Colleges 2009) are disheartening. Of roughly 13,000 interns who responded to the survey, 17% reported being publicly belittled or humiliated and, astonish-

ingly, 5% reported having been threatened with physical harm or physically punished (e.g., hit or slapped) during medical school. Most of the interns (56%) said that during medical school they were asked to perform
personal favors (e.g., shopping) by those in authority over them, and 5% had
been subjected to unwanted sexual advances. A sizeable minority of respondents also indicated that they were dissatisfied with the level of awareness and responsiveness of medical school administration regarding these issues in medical training.

    In another recent empirical study, 71 medical students were given a case
vignette in which a medical student rotating on a third-year clerkship was
reduced to tears while being questioned by the chairman of the department about a case that was handed off to the student a few minutes before.
Nearly one-third (32%) of the medical students who participated in the
survey thought that incidents like the one depicted in the vignette "were
to be expected in medicine," and 14% felt that the student in the scenario
had been "too sensitive." When commenting on whether she should write
up a complaint about the experience, the majority felt that it would be
seen as a sign of weakness and would hurt her chances for a good letter of
recommendation; a significant minority stated that it would adversely affect her grade and would "label her as a troublemaker." Another novel
study involving the qualitative analysis of ethical dilemmas reported by
medical students during their third year rotations revealed the theme of
mistreatment, with the patient most commonly being the "recipient of
unfair, disrespectful, insensitive, or cold/inhumane treatment" but students
also sharing in this difficult experience. As noted by Kelly and Nisker
(2009), "the clinical clerk was the second-most-frequent target"—behind
patients, sadly—for mistreatment, and they provided this student narrative
elicited in their study: "The senior [resident] that I was working under was
very tough on all the clerks, but in particular on one of my colleagues.
While I felt that it was unfair of the senior to consistently demean, single
out, and belittle that clerk in front of everyone else, if I spoke up in his
defense, then I'd become the new scapegoat."

    This latter study, published in 2009, suggests the close tie between mis-
treatment of patients and of clinical "subordinates," particularly in high-
stress, demanding inpatient settings. It further suggests that there is a long
distance to travel in assuring that clinical care and training settings support
positive and respectful behaviors. It appears that the culture of mistreatment
and silence continues (Ahmer et al. 2009; Coverdale et al. 2009; Heru et al.
2009), and it sadly gives rise to disruptive physicians of the future.

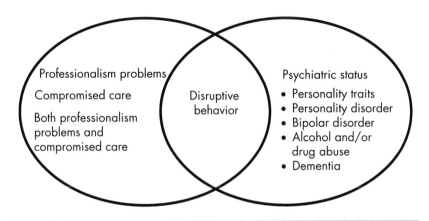

FIGURE 8–1.   **Disruptive behavior.**

Understanding and Managing the Disruptive Physician

Disruptive physicians exhibit a broad range of behaviors that have multiple causes (see Figure 8–1). The emphasis in this chapter is on the way that psychiatrists treat those with whom they work. However, we wish to emphasize that these professionalism problems may also involve outright incompetent treatment or questionable decision making. The case of Dr. Alberts that opens Chapter 1 is an example of such an individual. Hence a physician or psychiatrist who is disruptive could have problems only in the area of professionalism, have difficulties that compromise patient care, or engage in behavior that encompasses both categories (see Figure 8–1).

In a similar vein, there are a variety of reasons that the doctor might be disruptive in the workplace. Some of these individuals have no psychiatric diagnosis but have certain ways of reacting to stress, dealing with conflict, or approaching those in subordinate positions that are habitual patterns of relatedness. These behaviors may be entrenched personality traits, but they fall short of true personality disorder. Others will have longstanding characterological features, such as impulsivity, irritability or a "short fuse," poor judgment, narcissistic rage, and a proneness to treat others with contempt that have led to chronic problems in both love and work and will clearly place them in the category of one or another personality disorder.

Substance abuse or even isolated situations of excessive alcohol intake often lie behind the manifestations of unprofessional behavior. A long-standing humorous definition of the superego is "that part of the brain that is soluble in alcohol." Some psychiatrists will behave in ways that cause them to be mortified retrospectively because they were intoxicated or under the influence of drugs. Their behavior may be disruptive only when they are intoxicated, and they otherwise comport themselves with admirable decorum.

On the other hand, disruptive behavior may be governed by an underlying psychiatric diagnosis. For instance, bipolar disorder may also be responsible for disruptive and unprofessional behavior during a hypomanic or manic episode. In the aging physician, one may see early signs of dementia leading to unprofessional behavior. Frontal lobe involvement for reasons other than aging may also disinhibit doctors and lead them to make impulsive and hurtful comments or behave in ways that are disturbing to others.

We provide this context for understanding the problems that occur in interpersonal relationships in psychiatric practice to make a central point about disruptive behavior—namely, some of the behaviors commonly labeled as "unprofessional" may be refractory to seminars in professionalism training because they are directly related to significant underlying psychopathology. In such situations, the behavior may not improve or abate in the absence of an accurate diagnosis and adequate psychiatric intervention. The underlying causes of disruptive behavior must be assessed, and complex decisions about fitness for duty may have to be made by an evaluating psychiatrist. Figure 8–2 suggests how one might proceed with a series of questions. Are there psychiatric or substance abuse issues present? If so, what are they and what kind of treatment is necessary? Is long-term psychotherapy needed to increase mentalizing capacity, along with workplace monitoring that involves systematic feedback from coworkers? Or is short-term treatment sufficient? If treatment does not help, there may need to be administrative or professional consequences. If no psychiatric issues are present, one needs to decide if the problems are transient or enduring. If transient, are there system issues, such as splitting or other group dynamics, that need to be addressed? If the issues are enduring, limit setting, education, and workplace monitoring can be implemented. If there is no improvement, disciplinary measures, such as termination of employment, or administrative changes, such as moving personnel, may be required (see Figure 8–2). When an entire system is dysfunctional, sometimes an organizational consultant is useful.

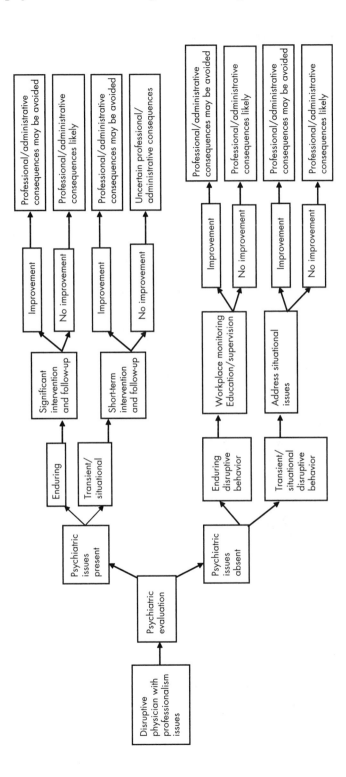

FIGURE 8–2. Disruptive physicians assessment.

Fitness for Duty

One of the quandaries presented in cases of disruptive colleagues is whether or not the individual is capable of practicing without jeopardizing patient safety. This determination may be necessary after initial complaints have been filed, or it may arise *after* the colleague has been through a rehabilitation or treatment program. Regardless of whether the individual has a psychiatric disturbance or not, expert opinion may be required to determine if returning to work will jeopardize either patient care or the work environment itself by placing coworkers in a difficult situation. A number of psychological characteristics need to be assessed that will assist in making this determination (see Table 8–1).

Although the psychological factors depicted in Table 8–1 may not cover all contingencies, they are a sampling of the kinds of considerations that those who are evaluating colleagues must take into account. The use of drugs and alcohol could impact many of these areas, whereas certain psychiatric disorders may only cause problems in discrete areas. For example, a psychiatrist with untreated attention-deficit/hyperactivity disorder may have difficulties with pace and persistence but otherwise function well. Other colleagues may have problems in areas such as reliability or persistence because of innate personality traits that fall short of the threshold for a psychiatric diagnosis. A detailed account of the complexities of physician evaluation is beyond the scope of this chapter but can be found elsewhere (see Myers and Gabbard 2008).

There are three possible outcomes following a fitness for duty evaluation: 1) the physician is fit to return to work with no restrictions because the individual has fully resolved the relevant problems; 2) the physician is fit to return to work with restrictions or modifications; or 3) the physician is unfit to return to practice. In cases that fall under category 2, the physician appears to be clinically competent and able to work as a physician safely and behave in a professional manner if certain treatments or external structures are put into place. These may involve workplace monitoring, medication, psychotherapy, random urine drug screenings, attendance at 12-step groups, professionalism education, mentoring, supervision, or change of work setting. In the case of category 3, there may be conditions such as dementia that may preclude someone from ever returning to a status where they would be fit for duty. On the other hand, there could be intractable characterological features that make it impossible for the colleague to get along with others.

TABLE 8–1. **Psychological factors relevant to fitness for duty**

Psychological factors	Effects on job performance
Cognition	Intelligence, memory, and executive functioning
Pace	The ability to perform tasks at an appropriate speed
Persistence	The ability to maintain attention and stay with a task until it is complete
Reliability	Coming to work every day in spite of personal or emotional problems; returning pages and phone calls in a timely manner
Conscientiousness and motivation	Wanting and trying to do a good job
Interpersonal functioning	The ability to accept supervision and to get along with coworkers and patients; the capacity for empathy and compassion with patients
Honesty, trustworthiness	The ability to be truthful, direct, and straightforward; taking responsibility when a mistake is made; maintaining professional boundaries with colleagues and patients
Stress tolerance	The ability to withstand job pressures (transference, night call, abuse stories, suicide, risk of violence) and to work with difficult people
Mentalizing capacity	Having the capacity to appreciate that the perspective of another person is different than one's own
Impulsivity and judgment	The capacity to remain level headed, delay knee-jerk responses, and anticipate the consequences of one's actions

Hierarchical Relationships and Power Imbalance

Just as we accept the fact that there is a power imbalance inherent in the doctor-patient relationship, we also know that such power differentials exist in interprofessional relationships. Physicians are often at the top of the hierarchy of a hospital or outpatient clinic team, yet they may be unaware of that status and how it influences the reactions of others to them in the course of the work day.

> Dr. Pollock, a 57-year-old psychiatrist, was referred for evaluation by the peer review committee of the veterans' hospital where he had worked for many years. He was respected as a clinician, and he was generally liked and valued by his patients because they sensed that he cared about them and was doing his best to treat their conditions. He was the director of a trauma unit where he had treated many combat veterans and had developed considerable expertise in that area.
>
> On the other hand, he had had rocky relationships with many of his coworkers for decades, and complaints against him had finally brought him to the point where the peer review committee felt an outside evaluation was warranted. An incident that served as a kind of tipping point occurred in a meeting of the multidisciplinary staff on his unit. A relatively young social worker on the team had broken down in tears and run out of a group meeting in the hospital unit when one of the veterans spoke in detail about a dramatic experience he had witnessed. In the staff meeting that occurred later that day, Dr. Pollock upbraided the social worker in front of the other unit staff: "This treatment unit is not about you and your vulnerabilities. You have to be there for the patients in that group. If you're so fragile that you can't handle the stress of the job, you can always look elsewhere for employment." Other members in the staff meeting looked at the floor and said nothing. When the meeting was over, the social worker told Dr. Pollock that she felt publicly humiliated by him and did not appreciate the way he had handled the situation. She acknowledged that it was not a good idea to break down in tears in front of the patients, but she told him that if he had advice or feedback for her, she preferred to hear it in private. He replied, "I'm not here to hold your hand or babysit you. This is a tough job, and if you can't stand the heat, get out of the kitchen." This kind of interaction had been recurrent throughout the time that he was on the unit. Some of the team had gotten used to him and supported him. Others had found him impossible and asked to be transferred. Those who had left his unit complained that he was abrupt, rude, insensitive, and unnecessarily blunt.

When a new chief was appointed to lead the mental health division, Dr. Pollock's actions and "style of leadership" were quickly brought to her attention by the chair of the peer review committee. The chair had heard about Dr. Pollock but was frustrated because there were many rumors but few actual formal complaints about him. The new chief reviewed the personnel file, which revealed little about the overall set of issues but did suggest a pattern of worrisome behavior. She then spoke with staff members who worked closely with Dr. Pollock. She recognized that he was an important and tireless worker over many years in the mental health division but also concluded that the behavior was problematic and perhaps worsening. She recommended that Dr. Pollock be seen for a psychiatric evaluation to determine his fitness for duty. He was referred to a psychiatrist working with a multidisciplinary team outside of the organization.

Dr. Pollock underwent a full workup, and no Axis I diagnosis was evident. One concern the evaluation team had was that he might have become more disinhibited recently because of cognitive-based deterioration. Nevertheless, neuropsychological testing indicated that he was cognitively intact.

One of the psychiatrists on his evaluation team went over some of the complaints with him, and Dr. Pollock responded in the following manner: "It is so ironic that they are concerned about my professionalism. It's exactly because of unprofessional behavior in *other* staff members that I get into trouble. If somebody jumps up in the middle of the meeting, bursts into tears, and runs out of the room, that person needs to be confronted. That type of behavior is unacceptable. She's a professional, and she needs to behave professionally." The psychiatrist then asked him if there is a way that he could give feedback to his fellow workers without creating bad feelings that lead people to resign. Dr. Pollock responded, "I'm not going to change the way I run my unit. Some people should *not* be working there because they can't cut the mustard. I did my psychiatric residency in the military, and I learned a certain way of relating to those who fall below expectations. I've used it for years, and it's worked very well. I can't tell you how many people have thanked me for the way I trained them."

The evaluating psychiatrist then asked if it bothered him that the peer review committee thought he was functioning so poorly that they placed him on administrative leave to get an evaluation. Dr. Pollock clarified with a discussion of the institutional politics: "You don't know the history of the conflict between the chief of the peer review committee and me. He has never liked me, and he has always felt very competitive with me. He saw this most recent incident as an opportunity to stab me in the back, and that's exactly what he's doing. He's the one who really ought to be here."

This vignette clearly suggests that mentalization problems are at the core of Dr. Pollock's professionalism difficulties. He cannot see that his perspective on situations is just one of many. He particularly has trouble recognizing the impact he has on others with his heavy-handed behavior, and he does not fully appreciate the hierarchical nature of the relationships on his unit. He understands that he is in charge and is authorized to supervise others, but he does not recognize how intimidating and bullying he is in the way he exercises his authority. Because of the power differential, when he says something to someone with whom he works, it is not simply "feedback" but an experience of devastating public humiliation. Although there may be areas of conflict with people in administrative positions, such as the chair of the peer review committee, Dr. Pollock also externalizes all of the difficulties that have occurred around him over the years and cannot see his own contributions to the situations that lead to complaints. He subsequently acknowledged that he had observed this kind of behavior in his early formative years from his superiors and understood that such behavior was acceptable.

Because the pattern was long-standing, Dr. Pollock may be less malleable and have a great reluctance to change how he manages a unit. In such a situation, an organization that wishes to promote a positive culture must recognize how this goal will only be attained if Dr. Pollock's behavior is addressed. As an attending physician of standing, Dr. Pollock influences the experiences of others in his workplace. If he is permitted to continue without consequence, then no amount of "sensitivity training" sessions will create a more positive culture. The "talk" and the "walk" of an organization must be aligned in order to introduce and sustain positive values in the workplace. However, others may be more responsive to feedback from helpful mentors or colleagues, both within and outside the system.

In the training of psychiatrists, there needs to be an emphasis on the bidirectional context of supervision so that the supervisor learns from the supervisee. Different supervisees require different strategies to maximize learning. One must find ways to provide feedback in a constructive manner so that it is actually implemented by the person in the lower position of the hierarchical structure. Moreover, negative feedback must be given in private rather than in public settings.

Whereas Dr. Pollock's behavior is more overt and obnoxious, there are many subtle ways that power issues emerge in workplace settings that lead to difficulties in cohesive teamwork, whether in outpatient clinics or inpatient settings. Bradshaw (1972), for instance, wrote a classic paper about the interaction of coworkers on a psychiatric hospital unit. A crisis within the staff group emerged when one of the residents complained that no one had made coffee one morning. One of the mental health technicians responded that anyone who wanted coffee should make it for himself. As this was processed in a staff meeting, it became apparent that the coffee pot on the unit had become a symbol for who serves whom. Bradshaw pointed out that there are always a series of unspoken assumptions about who does what in multidisciplinary teams. There are often gender, racial, and ethnic issues that are embedded in hierarchies that lead people to feel they are being discriminated against because of skin color, gender, or socioeconomic status. Some female staff members on the unit thought coffee making was viewed as "women's work." Another issue that emerged in the discussion was the fact that different staff members were addressed differently (i.e., first names versus titles) depending on where they were situated within the unit hierarchy. Bradshaw stressed that those in the lower echelons of this hierarchy resented the inequality but were equally uncomfortable with being treated with more familiarity, such as calling one another by first names, because they did not want to assume greater responsibility or authority than their level of training.

Simple tasks such as making coffee for others, cleaning up a kitchen area, or handling paperwork can become a lightning rod for feelings of resentment, inequality, and powerlessness. Psychiatrists must develop an acute sensitivity to disenchantment among their coworkers and be willing to listen and offer ways of doing things differently within reason. Obviously, there is no substitute for showing respect for each coworker, regardless of position, and empathizing with the stress inherent in treating difficult patients.

Intercollegial Relationships

Dr. Harbarth, a psychiatrist , discovered that one of his patients had been seen by a psychologist colleague, Dr. Carlson, in the same multispecialty group practice while Dr. Harbarth was on vacation. The patient had come into the clinic very distressed on the day of his final court hearing related to a difficult and bitter divorce. The receptionist followed the clinic's usual procedure in these situations and called the psychiatrist on duty that day. She performed a quick assessment and referred the patient to the next available doctoral-level provider in their clinical practice—Dr. Carlson.

Dr. Carlson then performed a complete evaluation, quite concerned that the patient's psychosocial stresses associated with the divorce revealed a more serious set of mental health issues than had been identified in his routine care. The patient was given a different diagnosis, and the psychologist recommended immediate supportive therapy and suggested that longer-term cognitive-behavioral therapy may be appropriate. Dr. Carlson indicated in his report that these psychosocial interventions should be offered in addition to the medications prescribed by Dr. Harbarth.

The patient understood that Dr. Carlson had "stepped in" for Dr. Harbarth while he was on vacation. The patient asked Dr. Carlson if he could continue in the care of *both* Dr. Carlson and Dr. Harbarth. He said, "Dr. Harbarth is great at the medicines, but he doesn't really listen. It's really helped me to work with you too. I don't want to quit seeing Dr. Harbarth, and I don't want to hurt his feelings. He's been a good doctor to me. But you are too! Can't we do both?"

When Dr. Harbarth learned of the psychologist visits from the receptionist, he became visibly agitated. "Carlson is a jerk—I can't believe this! This is so underhanded!" Dr. Harbarth then turned on his heels and stormed down the hall to the clinic scheduler and yelled, "That Carlson stole my patient, and he is completely incompetent! How could you let this happen?!" He paced around the scheduler's desk, which was adjacent to the patient waiting area. With a loud voice and noticeable sarcasm, he said, "Get Carlson on the phone NOW, and I don't care if he is 'in session'!" Then he muttered under his breath, "These psychologists…they aren't even real doctors" and returned angrily to his office down the hall.

Relationships between psychiatrists and other providers—whether psychologists, advanced practice nurses, fellow psychiatrists, or physicians in other specialties—deserve special consideration because of their complexity. It is impossible to understand intercollegial relatedness without examining the context of physician training. Medical and psychiatric training occurs in a competitive context. Consciously or unconsciously, one physician is frequently trying to outshine another physician. On hospital rounds during medical school and residency training, the trainee who gives the right answer most rapidly is admired, envied, and respected. He or she may also be resented. Similarly, psychologists and advance practice nurses undergo very rigorous and lengthy preparation. These training paths are not immune to the same competitive pressures as physician training. Moreover, these talented and high-achieving professionals may find themselves in medical settings where their roles are less clear and their discipline's contributions are less highly valued, creating distinct tensions in their interprofessional interactions.

When one physician is consulting on a patient seen by another subspecialist physician, a wish to "one-up" the treating physician is often enacted in covert or overt ways that are designed to put the consultant in favorable light and the consultee in the shadow of the consultant. There is an unfortunate tradition in academic medical centers of regarding a referring physician who is outside academia as the "LMD," which stands for "local medical doctor," a pejorative term implying that a busy physician in private practice is either less clinically sophisticated than the academic consultant or less informed by the literature. Similar challenges exist for clinical caregivers when their patients are seen by consultants, teammates, and cross-covering professionals in the community-based healthcare systems.

Busy practitioners who are not affiliated with academic institutions may, in turn, look at the academics as ivory-tower intellectuals who are entirely out of touch with the vicissitudes of psychiatric practice. They may feel that much of their perspective on a patient is far too idealistic to implement in a private practice setting. They may also feel (often with good reason) that they are being looked down upon, and they assume that the findings of a consultant are inherently a criticism of the referring clinician.

Some patients who are referred from one psychiatrist to another for consultation are either consciously or unconsciously aware of the potential rivalry between the two physicians. The patient may ventilate about perceived deficiencies in the treating psychiatrist, and it is incumbent upon the consultant to maintain a professional attitude where he or she does not join in the devaluation of the treating doctor. One can listen empathically without agreeing that the psychiatrist involved in the treatment of the patient is somehow neglectful or incompetent. There is no substitute for mutual respect in the context of consultations of this sort.

Intercollegial relationships also can be characterized by lax standards of confidentiality. As noted in Chapter 3, some psychiatrists love to gossip about an important patient they see, whereas others love to drop hints about the wealth or status of their patients. Still others love to talk about "an interesting case" they are seeing. These interchanges often grow out of the same competitiveness described earlier, but they also border on being unethical in their tendency to throw confidentiality to the winds. Enough can be said about a patient that a colleague will recognize the identity of that patient. In formal consultation, psychiatrists need to follow the standard operating procedure regarding release of information to ensure the patient that confidentiality is respected. At times, a patient may refuse to give consent for the psychiatrist to talk to the referring psychiatrist, and the consultant must respect that the patient's wish for confidentiality trumps the psychiatrist's wish to communicate with the colleague. Obviously, in some forensic settings, the issue of confidentiality does not apply because a third party has requested an evaluation. In those settings, if a patient refuses to sign a consent for the evaluator to talk, then the evaluation cannot proceed.

When psychiatrists are consulting for other physicians in medical and surgical specialties, they are often mocked and teased as not being "real doctors." Psychiatrists may joke about colleagues as having "surgical personalities" or "zero psychological mindedness." This sparring across specialties has been a source of a great deal of unprofessional behavior that often carries into gossiping about colleagues in the hospital cafeteria or the doctors' lounge. Even though such behavior is ubiquitous, it is still unprofessional. Nothing gains more respect for a psychiatrist than doing a competent job of consulting and speaking with the referring doctor in a respectful way.

Group and Institutional Dynamics

As noted earlier in this chapter, the problems that occur in the workplace setting often transcend the consideration of one individual. Psychiatric institutions and other mental health settings constitute a system that must be taken into account. Certain group and institutional dynamics operate consistently in such settings and influence professionalism. A cornerstone of psychodynamic psychiatry is that people behave differently in groups than they do in a one-on-one situation (Gabbard 2005). Hence many problems in professionalism must also be conceptualized systemically. A clinical example illuminates this notion in greater detail.

> Alice, a 24-year-old patient with borderline personality disorder, had been hospitalized for suicidal behavior in a private psychiatric hospital. She had stormy relationships with some of the staff while interacting harmoniously with others. The disparity with which she was viewed by the various members of the treatment team led to considerable conflict. In one instance, she was discovered by a nurse, Ms. Smith, standing in front of the television set in the unit lounge bleeding from both forearms, where she had cut her-

self. Ms. Smith arranged for her to be sutured by the doctor on call. The next day, in a meeting of the staff members involved in her treatment team, Ms. Smith ventilated her anger: "I'm so furious at Alice. I can't believe she would be so deceptive. I asked her if she had any sharp objects in her room, and she told me emphatically that she did not. She even said that she didn't appreciate being accused by me in that way. Now I find out that she has a razor blade hidden in a light fixture in her room and used that to cut herself. She looked me in the eye and lied to me!"

Dr. Covalt, the team psychologist, felt provoked by Ms. Smith's comments and made the following statement: "I think *you* need to look at your own contribution to what happened." Ms. Smith was caught off guard by the comment and asked with irritation in her voice: "Are you saying that I'm responsible for her cutting?" Dr. Covalt responded, "Well, all I'm saying, is that Alice feels that she cannot get your attention because you're always busy when she wants to talk to you. It may be that cutting herself is the only way to engage you." This allegation made Ms. Smith furious, and she attacked Dr. Covalt: "Well, that's easy for you to say. You're not on the unit with the patients 8 hours a day like I am. All you do is sit on your ass and write testing reports and drink coffee." Dr. Covalt escalated the altercation further: "You have to understand. Alice has been subjected to unspeakably horrific childhood trauma, and she has to be made to feel that she is special and valued. You can't treat her like just one of the patients who can wait around forever to talk to you." Ms. Smith then rose from her chair and said, "My shift is over, and I'm going home. And frankly, I don't need you to tell me how to do my job."

The rest of the treatment team looked stunned as the meeting ended, and tension lingered in the air for 2 days until the next staff meeting. At this meeting, the psychiatrist team leader pointed out that both Ms. Smith and Dr. Covalt were competent and intelligent members of the treatment team. He tried to bring an educational focus to the session. He pointed out that the phenomenon of "splitting," so common in borderline personality disorder, had divided Ms. Smith and Dr. Covalt into a "good object" and a "bad object." Alice treated Ms. Smith with contempt while idealizing Dr. Covalt. With the passage of 48 hours, both Ms. Smith and Dr. Covalt were able to reflect a bit on the pattern that the team leader was describing. Dr. Covalt acknowledged that Alice did relate to him as an idealized father who was something of a rescuer. He openly acknowledged, "There's no question that I feel protective of her and want to assure that she gets the best treatment that she can." Ms. Smith was not as willing to acknowledge her part, but she certainly could see that she was consistently treated as the villain in the patient's treatment narrative and did not like being in that role.

The countertransferences that occur in psychotherapy occur in all treatment settings. In this case, the splitting was augmented by projective identification in that Alice treated Ms. Smith as "all bad" and Dr. Covalt as "all good" (Gabbard 1989, 1994). In each case, the person receiving the projections became colonized by the projections and felt transformed into what was being projected through the interpersonal pressure of the patient. In other words, they were enacting the bad or good object that had been thrust upon them by Alice. Hence the unprofessional behavior witnessed in the staff meeting reflected the psychopathology of the patient and the preexisting differences with the team about treatment philosophy. In fact, Ms. Smith and Dr. Covalt had been on the opposite ends of splitting maneuvers before, and they gradually began to realize their vulnerability to these roles over time. Splitting in multiple-treater settings often revolves around one person who is strictly adherent to hospital policies, procedures, and structure and another who is more lax about such things and believes in individualizing treatment (Gabbard 1989, 1994).

In any case, unprofessional behavior in an institution needs to take into account the group forces that operate. Both Ms. Smith and Dr. Covalt were entirely reasonable people when approached on a one-to-one basis. Forces such as scapegoating and spokesperson phenomena are commonplace, however, and one needs to be aware of the role suction of group dynamics that can make a person feel coerced into fulfilling a certain role for the group (Gabbard 2005). As in all of psychiatry, countertransference influences as well as group factors must be taken into account if we are to fully understand unprofessional behavior.

Although this vignette occurs in the context of the group dynamics of a hospital team, large groups coexist with small groups in hospital settings and academic training centers as well as in any other kind of institutional work in nonhospital settings. One must be cognizant of how mental health professionals who feel beleaguered in a system under strain may also begin to enact various roles that lead to unprofessional behavior and demeaning comments. Often these comments are directed toward people in powerful positions in the institution, reflecting the professional sense of helplessness to change a system in which they work or the society responsible for funding mental healthcare. Those colleagues in administrative positions are out of sight to a large extent and therefore are easy scapegoats for the ventilation of one's own feelings of powerlessness. As we have noted before, one is entitled to whatever feelings he or she may have, but such feelings can be expressed through appropriate channels where differences of opinion can be aired constructively.

Toward a Solution

Attempting to address the professionalism problems noted in this chapter related to interprofessional interactions is a daunting task. As a professional working within an organization, it is important to understand the relevant policies related to professional conduct, sexual harassment, disruptive behavior, and impairment. Ideally, the organization will have steps that can be undertaken as problem behavior is first being identified and addressed, permitting the physician to rectify his or her actions in the workplace. More serious consequences may need to be introduced if the behaviors are particularly egregious, but often busy, conscientious, and exhausted clinicians may not understand the effects of their behavior. Provision of objective feedback alone may be sufficient to improve the situation.

Preventive measures, of course, are far better than contemplating treatment approaches. Role models in the work setting who value professionalism are essential. Routine processes for providing feedback to professionals regarding the observable strengths and weaknesses they may have in the domain of interprofessional interactions are extremely important—such processes help professionals to understand the impact they have upon others and to recall the influence and power they possess in their roles. These routine processes help deescalate the shame involved in receiving an occasional negative comment from colleagues, and they help to communicate the importance of interprofessional interactions in the eyes of the organization. Education in clinical seminars can be helpful as well. Complex situations can be examined from the standpoint of multiple determinants to train psychiatrists and other mental health professionals to think in depth about professionalism problems that they may encounter in practice.

In addition to formal education, a number of principles can be implemented in work settings that help promote positive working relationships. We are not so naive to think that an attempt to adhere to these principles will eradicate unprofessional behavior, but they serve as guideposts to help one through the complex and often chaotic day-to-day crises that occur in psychiatric settings.

1. Treat colleagues and coworkers as valued individuals who deserve to have their points of view listened to and validated.

2. Respond promptly to calls or pages from those with whom you work and show up for meetings on time. Both behaviors indicate respect for others.
3. Make a point of trying to mentalize a coworker's perspective on a situation, recognizing that it may be different from one's own but equally legitimate.
4. Be aware of competitiveness and try to minimize this disruptive effect on the working relationships.
5. Always be aware of the hierarchical nature of the work setting and the power differential that is present even when you think it is not operating.
6. Remember that racial and ethnic issues may be the most difficult ones to talk about and may be undercurrents in working groups that are never discussed but are secretly observed by all.
7. Give feedback toward others in private so that it can be heard without the effects of public humiliation.
8. Be aware that strong emotional reactions occurring toward others may be influenced by individual patients and group/institutional dynamics that are largely unconscious.

Key Points

- **Professionalism encompasses the expectation of sensitive and respectful behavior toward all colleagues and coworkers despite the stresses of the work setting.**

- **Evidence from diverse sources indicates that disruptive physician behavior is widely prevalent. The culture of mistreatment and silence in demanding inpatient training settings appears to continue, with patients and trainees being the most likely recipients of this unacceptable behavior.**

- **Disruptive behavior is defined by the American Medical Association as "personal conduct, whether verbal or physical, that negatively affects or that potentially may negatively affect patient care..."**

- **A physician who is disruptive could have problems only in the area of professionalism, have difficulties only in the area of** compromised patient care, or engage in behavior that encompasses both categories.

- There are multiple reasons why a doctor may be disruptive in the workplace. Therefore, the mechanisms utilized to address the disruptive behavior must be tailored to the needs of the individual. Of particular importance is that education on professionalism alone is not the answer.

- If a physician is found to be disruptive, there needs to be a determination regarding whether or not the individual is fit for duty.

- Just as we accept the fact that there is a power imbalance inherent in the doctor-patient relationship, we also know that such power differentials exist in interprofessional relationships, where physicians are often at the top of the hierarchy of the team. Physicians must be aware of that status and how it influences the reactions of others to them.

- Psychiatrists must develop an acute sensitivity to disenchantment among their coworkers and be willing to listen and offer ways of doing things differently within reason.

- Sparring across specialties has been a source of a great deal of unprofessional behavior. Even though such behavior is ubiquitous, it is still unprofessional.

- Countertransference influences, as well as group dynamics, must be taken into account if we are to fully understand unprofessional behavior.

- Prevention begins with role models who value professionalism. Other essential preventive measures include awareness of an institution's relevant policies related to professional conduct, sexual harassment, disruptive behavior, and impairment and the provision of feedback to professionals regarding the observable strengths and weaknesses they have in the domain of interprofessional interactions.

Chapter 9

Light and Shadow in the "Hidden Curriculum"

The setting is a small conference room on a psychiatric inpatient unit in a general hospital. Huddled around the conference room are six post-graduate year (PGY)–III psychiatric residents, three third-year medical students, a psychology intern, and two psychiatric nurses. At the head of the table sits Dr. Stapleton, a psychiatrist who has served as an inpatient attending for more than 20 years. He stares blankly as Dr. Zachary, one of the PGY-III residents, presents his workup of the recently admitted psychiatric patient to him. Dr. Stapleton listens to the presentation while clicking the top of a ballpoint pen in and out. Dr. Zachary periodically looks up from his notes at Dr. Stapleton, only to see a kind of deadness in his professor's eyes that makes him worry that his presentation is falling short of expectations. Dr. Zachary continues with the presentation and describes the patient's medication history: "I don't think there's any question that the patient is depressed. It's puzzling that she hasn't responded to medications. She's had two different SSRIs at reasonable doses, and one of them was tried in conjunction with Wellbutrin, and there wasn't much of a change in her depression. It is my feeling that she ought to be given a course of ECT while she's here in the unit."

Dr. Stapleton interrupts at this point and asks rather harshly, "It was your *feeling?*" Dr. Zachary hesitates for a moment and responds, "Yes, it was my feeling that maybe ECT should be tried now." Dr. Stapleton then raises his voice and stops clicking his ballpoint pen: "What on Earth do you think you're doing bringing your feelings to a conference of physicians about a patient with a serious psychiatric illness?" Dr. Zachary tries to mount a feeble answer, but Dr. Stapleton continues, "We have taught you a clear algorithm for using medication treatment for refractory depression, including which classes of medications to try, when to augment, when to switch, and dosage range and duration. Yet you come to a conference of physicians with a half-baked history that tells us almost nothing about what has been tried so far, and you have the nerve to say it's your *feeling* that maybe ECT should be tried! If you think ECT is indicated, you need to present a persuasive, clinical, and scientific case for why ECT is indicated. We are not interested in your feelings." Dr. Zachary turns crimson and does not know what to say. Dr. Stapleton stands up and says, "I'm going to end the conference now. After you have the data you need, page me and we'll talk again." He strides out of the conference room into the corridor of the inpatient unit, leaving the trainees behind him dismayed, stunned, and unsure what to do next. Finally, one of the medical students says, "I guess he got up on the wrong side of the bed today." A third-year resident who has watched the debacle from start to finish casually notes, "No, not really. Stapleton thinks that's the way you learn."

This group of aspiring psychiatrists and other mental health professionals has just witnessed a form of teaching by shaming and humiliating. They have also observed a professor in the psychiatry department treat a younger colleague with contempt without regard for his feelings or the impact of such treatment on his professional growth. This form of treatment is an extreme variation on what is commonly known as "pimping" (Detsky 2009), a long-standing tradition in medical education where an attending physician shames a resident or medical student by posing questions in a way that is intended to expose the trainee's lack of knowledge rather than bring forward information or learning. The power relationship is misused in such situations—the attending seeks to assert his or her superiority over another, gratifying his own needs rather than fulfilling professional responsibilities. Like fraternity or sorority hazing, it establishes a precedent that others may pass on when they are in powerful positions over subordinates, hence assuring that teaching by shaming and humiliating will continue through the ages. As stated eloquently by McKegney (1989), "Like parents who raise their children as they themselves were raised, each generation (in medicine) teaches as they were taught, and the patterns are loyally perpetuated" (p. 452).

This psychiatric residency did not have a seminar that taught the art of pimping. The residents and medical students were learning how to treat colleagues and trainees simply by watching a senior colleague explode with contempt during a conference on an inpatient teaching unit. In other words, they were not learning from a formal curriculum but from an informal or "hidden" curriculum. They were reminded once again of the gap between what is taught in the classroom about professionalism and how role models actually conduct themselves in a clinical or an educational setting. Dr. Stapleton may have been treated that way when he was a resident and thus internalized that style of teaching to ensure that residents come to case conferences well prepared. He probably had not stopped to think about the far-reaching influence that such behavior has on others.

Ultimately, this unfortunate episode in psychiatric education represents only one aspect of what has been referred to as "the hidden curriculum" of medical education. In a compelling commentary, a former president of the Association of American Medical Colleges lamented that the process of becoming a physician supports "aberrations in the moral and ethical behavior" of trainees. He cited, for instance, the competitiveness of pre-med students and the documented examples of misconduct of medical school applicants, for example, provision of faked transcripts and inauthentic letters of recommendation, as revealed through investigations performed by the Association. Petersdorf (1986) also described extensive data on cheating—in one study, a significant minority of students at one medical school admitted to cheating during college (33%–48%) and on medical school examinations (17%).

These findings align with the experiences of one of the authors of this book (L.W.R.), who administered a performance-based examination with standardized patients at one medical school; the examination was videotaped, and several students were "caught red-handed" looking at notes that were "smuggled" into the examination (Roberts et al. 1999). Unpublished results of an attitude survey with students at this same school regarding academic misconduct (L.W. Roberts, T. McCarty, S.S. Obenshain, 1994–1999) revealed that students did not universally perceive "faking the results of a laboratory experiment," "asking another student for exam answers," "permitting another student to look at your answer sheet during a quiz," "working in a group on a homework assignment that was assigned as individual work," and "delaying taking an examination using a false excuse" as academic misconduct. Interestingly, every student indicated that taking an examination for another student was academic misconduct; it is distressing that only such a cut-and-dried misrepresentation is necessary for medical students to "see" misconduct.

Although the evidence suggests that earlier-career learners in medicine do not recognize and indeed may engage in unprofessional conduct, it appears that their more senior counterparts contribute to what has been described as a "neglectful and abusive family system" (McKegney 1989). It may be that faculty are responding to many stressors that exist in the current healthcare environment. A large study of 1,951 academic faculty at four medical schools (Schindler et al. 2006) revealed that 20% endorse significant depressive symptoms. Younger faculty members had a greater symptom burden, because they typically carry very heavy service responsibilities and experience genuine role tensions in caring for their families and addressing financial debt (Schindler et al. 2006). Work-related stresses were seen as the cause of mental health concerns and problems with job satisfaction, producing a situation in which faculty may be more vulnerable to unprofessional behavior and less able to rise above the negative culture they may experience in academic medical settings.

Some of the most admirable and enduring qualities of what it means to be a professional are also conveyed by modeling in a teaching setting. In fact, one could argue that most of what one learns about being a psychiatrist comes from informal interactions outside a formal curriculum. Some of the darkest moments in learning occur in these interactions with mentors and older trainees, but some of the most moving and compelling episodes are also ingrained in one's professional identity as well. Both light and shadow fall on the hidden curriculum.

Teaching Through Role Modeling

All physicians have their professional identity shaped by keeping their eyes and ears open as they start doing their clinical rotations in medical school and continue the process of learning in residencies and fellowships. They see that there is often a discrepancy between what is taught in the classroom and what actually plays out in interactions with patients and colleagues. Over time, each physician accumulates a set of narratives.

The cumulative impact of clinical incidents of training is consciously or unconsciously internalized. Some of these incidents are seared into the memory of the student in a way that haunts them.

Two medical students on an emergency department rotation worked feverishly with their attending in an effort to resuscitate an elderly woman who had had a myocardial infarction at home and had arrived in an ambulance. After nearly an hour of futile efforts, the attending decided that they had done their best and asked the students to come with him as he went out to the waiting room adjacent to the emergency department. The deceased patient's husband was pacing the floor but stopped abruptly when he saw the attending coming toward him, already reading his facial expression. The attending held the man by both elbows, looked directly into his eyes, and said, "Your wife didn't make it." The husband howled and exclaimed, "Our beautiful life together is over!" The attending continued to hold the man as he wept. He reassured him and said, "You did everything you possibly could. You called the ambulance and got her here as quickly as possible. You did nothing wrong." These two students noted that their mentor, himself feeling the intense pain of the moment, still managed to think about the husband's vulnerability to guilt feelings in the long run and was already attempting damage control so the husband did not end up blaming himself for his wife's death. The students never forgot this critical incident in their education; it was something they could have learned only "in the trenches" rather than in the classroom.

This vignette underscores the contrast between psychiatry and much of the rest of Western medicine. By its very nature, psychiatry requires greater privacy than most other specialties. Cardiopulmonary resuscitation in the emergency department is a quasi-public event. Much of psychiatric practice occurs behind closed doors in a one-to-one situation that is radically private. There are exceptions, of course, as in the inpatient unit case conference with Dr. Stapleton. Psychiatric residents often express a strong wish to see senior faculty evaluate or treat patients. In many educational settings, a one-way mirror is a highly valued teaching tool because trainees have the opportunity to see a mentor or teacher interact with a patient in a way that approximates the educator's actual clinical work. Videos used for teaching also are highly valued by those learning to be psychiatrists. Any way that training programs can set up opportunities for psychiatric residents to witness an attending interviewing a patient is certainly valuable from a professionalism standpoint.

Many of the narratives that have lasting impacts on the professional identity of psychiatrists happen serendipitously. One could even argue that planned interviews are more properly considered part of the *formal* curriculum. Encounters in the hidden curriculum are generally spontaneous rather than programmed.

Dr. Rosenberg, an associate professor who ran an outpatient teaching clinic in an academic department, was cleaning off her desk and finishing up her e-mails at 6:15 P.M. and trying to get out of the clinic to attend one of her children's basketball games with her husband. The phone rang, and it was the dean of student affairs of the medical school. She said she had a medical student in her office whom she was afraid was suicidal. The dean asked if she could send the student over for a brief evaluation because the dean, having trained in a surgical subspecialty, felt inadequate to assess suicidal risk. Dr. Rosenberg hesitated, thinking of her husband waiting for her and her child's basketball game, but she knew that someone needed to see the student and assess for danger to self. A life or death risk had to trump the basketball game. When she hung up the phone, she noticed a 4th-year resident standing in her doorway. Dr. Rosenberg asked what was wrong. The resident said that she just needed to get a prescription from her. The resident noted that Dr. Rosenberg seemed distressed as she wrote out a prescription for the resident's patient.

The resident asked if everything was okay. Dr. Rosenberg said that she was just frustrated because she was hoping to get out to meet her husband at 6:30 to go to their child's basketball game. The resident asked what was keeping her from it. She explained that one of the deans was sending her a student for evaluation. The resident said, "I'm sorry you have to be delayed like this. I wish I could see the patient for you, but since it's a student I probably shouldn't." Dr. Rosenberg smiled and said, "No, you really shouldn't. You'll get your chance one day." They both laughed. The resident, acutely aware of having to balance work and family in her own life, said to Dr. Rosenberg, "Do you ever regret being a doctor?" Dr. Rosenberg responded, "Not for one minute. I can come to the basketball game late, and my daughter will understand. There will also be 10 or 12 more basketball games before the season's over. This student's life may hang in the balance. This is why I became a doctor. Now why don't you get yourself home?"

The resident left and thought about her experience on the drive home. She looked back on it years later as a formative moment in her professional identity because the whole incident brought home the reality that it was impossible to perfectly balance work and family. An even greater lesson was the message that Dr. Rosenberg imparted to her about the values inherent in medicine and psychiatric practice. She often summoned that moment from her memory when she was in a stressful situation. That internalized image of Dr. Rosenberg facing a difficult situation at the end of the day with altruism and dedication was a beacon in the darkness for the rest of her career.

Dr. Rosenberg's example brought home to her trainee what she *actually* did rather than what was taught in the classroom about what one *should* do.

Dr. Rosenberg's example underscores the fact that psychiatry, like all medical practice, is a moral undertaking that must be taken seriously (Inui 2003). In an era in which much is made of healthcare financing and the need for medicine to be cost effective, doctors often complain about decreased income and loss of prestige. A great deal is written about virtue and the moral imperative to care for those who need it, even at considerable sacrifice to the self. An overarching component of professionalism is doing the right thing in the right circumstances. The best that we can hope for with psychiatric educators is to model that behavior in day-to-day situations for those who are training to become psychiatrists.

Distinct Ethical Tensions in the Hidden Curriculum of Psychiatry Residency Training

The ethical tensions inherent in the hidden curriculum of psychiatry residency are many and difficult to navigate, particularly in relation to four aspects of training, as noted by Lane (1990) and by Hoop (2004). The first relates to assuming the identity, stance, and skill set as a practicing psychiatrist. The second relates to ethical conflicts that arise when one is both a learner and a caregiver whose education and work entail the "use" of patients. The third pertains to the resident as both a physician and a supervisee, and the fourth relates to the resident as both a learner and an employee within a larger system.

In becoming a psychiatrist, the resident becomes privy to the intimate world of patients, and in this process, the resident reflects on complex issues that range from definitions of "health" and normality versus "illness" and pathology to transference and countertransference. The psychiatric resident undergoes the experience of placing patients on "holds" or administering medications against the wishes of patients who are severely symptomatic and dangerous to themselves and others, an awesome and awful role in which one encroaches upon the liberties of another human being. The resident may be the victim of threats, assault, "stalking," and other invasions of his or her privacy quite unexpectedly in training. Less dramatically, every resident has "diagnosed" friends, family, neighbors, colleagues, and celebrities while reading through DSM and major textbooks in the field, leaving the resident with doubts and hard questions about his or her upbringing, relationships, and future. More difficult is recognizing different traits (e.g., perfectionism) or defenses (e.g., displacement) that typify some of the personality disorders or are hallmarks of major mental disorders, such as depression or anxiety. Furthermore, an intentional part of psychiatry training is to help the early career psychiatrist learn a sense of skepticism, balance, and objectivity in observing one's own reactions and behavior. There is a division of self that occurs in this process. Finally, the resident becomes exhausted by the work load and service requirements, the proximity to suffering, and the effort involved in interacting with many different patients, family members, and professional staff in the new role as "the doctor." Just as the nature of becoming a surgeon who literally cuts into the bodies of patients creates distinct ethical tensions for some early career physicians, all of these features of assuming the professional role as a psychiatrist challenge and produce tensions in the forming identity of the psychiatric resident.

Being both a learner and a caregiver poses a second set of challenges. As Hoop (2004, p. 184) described, "psychiatrists-in-training provide treatment not just to benefit the patient, but also as a means of gaining clinical expertise"—something that stands in contrast to the goal of medicine and the ethical requirement "that doctors generally must consider patients as ends in themselves and not as means to another aim." She cited the example of a resident who performs a lumbar puncture for the first time or who provides care for a chronically suicidal patient for treatment despite her inexperience. The relative powerlessness of many psychiatric patients increases the ethical salience of this situation of competing concerns to learn and to provide care.

The third special consideration pertains to the relationship between the resident and the supervisor. Under the best of circumstances, when there is a good "fit" between these two professionals, there is the issue of divided responsibility in the care of patients. In addition, disagreements may arise between residents and supervisors, creating new ethical challenges that have to do with the fair resolution of the issue as well as commitment to the best interests of the patient. These concerns are greatest in "high risk situations," such as when a patient is potentially suicidal or gravely ill due to mental illness or when someone else's life and well-being are in jeopardy.

Although there are role conflicts that arise for the resident as developing psychiatrist, as learner, as caregiver, and as supervisee, there are also special tensions that arise for the resident as an employee in the context of large organizations. Residents, who may be in their first formal job, must be compliant with the rules of the human resources department, the legal office, and the billing office. They may be required to enforce policies that are uncomfortable, and they may need to represent the institution in new settings. Residents also may be for the first time in situations in which they must function effectively and with responsibility in team leadership or interprofessional duties, and their inexperience may lead to errors or boundary transgressions.

Taken together, these are very substantive concerns in the life of the resident, and yet the "hidden curriculum" may clearly indicate that the resident should minimize these challenges, not complain, and "get on with the work." The maturing psychiatrist, however, will seek to work through and integrate these aspects of his or her professional life. Excellent supervisors, throughout and after training, may help with this, as can consultative and collaborative work with colleagues.

Continuing Education and the Hidden Curriculum

One of the most far-reaching gratifications in the psychiatric profession is the opportunity to continue to grow and learn throughout one's professional life. In a similar way, professionalism is enhanced by our interactions with colleagues and mentors in those settings throughout the psychiatrist's career. One meets colleagues at national meetings and through peer referral networks that foster situations in which one learns from others on a continuing basis, not only from lectures but also from their modeling of professionalism. Some mentors are within one's own practice or academic environment, whereas others are geographically distant.

> Dr. Frost was an internationally renowned expert in bipolar disorder and was presenting some of the latest findings of clinical trials at a national meeting. After giving a stimulating lecture, he asked for questions from the audience. A member of the audience stood up in front of hundreds of psychiatrists in attendance at the lecture. He began speaking in the mi-

crophone as though he were going to ask a question. He began to complain vociferously about the medications he had received for his own bipolar illness, and it rapidly became apparent to everyone in the audience and to the lecturer that he was in either a hypomanic or manic episode and was going to continue to talk. Dr. Frost listened while the audience reacted with increasing distress. However, Dr. Frost tried to help the man in the audience to save face by asking him what medications he had tried. He listened sympathetically and empathized with the man how frustrating it was when there were so many agents that were used for the treatment of the illness but a relatively small amount of data.

After this dialogue had gone on for about 10 minutes, Dr. Frost, continuing to be respectful toward the man in the audience, said, "You know, you've been through a lot. Since the lecture's over, maybe you and I could chat for a bit over a cup of coffee and talk about this some more. I know they need this room for another event shortly." So he strode into the audience, shook the man's hand, and walked him out of the auditorium to everyone's relief. Throughout the interchange, Dr. Frost remained professional, concerned, and in no way humiliated the speaker. In fact, a number of attendees at the lecture saw him sitting with the man in a coffee shop after the lecture, continuing to engage in a constructive dialogue with the man about the treatment of bipolar illness.

Dr. Frost managed to handle a difficult situation in an unflappable way that all concerned thought was "a class act." At the same time, he modeled a professional role to an audience of colleagues that few ever forgot. He also drove the point home that even when one is outside of one's office in a setting where he is not seeing patients, one is still a psychiatrist and has a certain professional role that must be taken seriously.

All psychiatrists benefit from observing and internalizing the way colleagues relate to them in a variety of different experiences that they encounter in their professional careers. One of the most difficult things to endure is the suicide of a patient, and the way colleagues respond may serve as a template for the way a psychiatrist who loses a patient treats future colleagues in similar distressing moments. There are no guidelines to follow in such situations, but reaching out rather than shunning one's colleague can have a very powerful effect.

> Dr. Menken worked in a private clinic with seven colleagues with whom he shared a large section of their building. He frequently chatted between appointments and at the end of the day. One afternoon in October, Dr. Menken's assistant received a call from a sobbing husband who said his wife had killed herself. The wife had been a patient of Dr. Menken's. Dr. Menken quickly got on the phone and tried to comfort the

grieving husband. He told him that he would be glad to help in any way he could. It was 5:00, and Dr. Menken had another patient to see, but he had his assistant Janice tell the patient that he would have to reschedule the appointment because something had come up. Dr. Menken sat stunned in his desk chair from the unexpected news of the suicide. There was a knock at the door, and it was a female colleague about his age who worked down the hall from him. She asked if she could come in, and he said, "Sure." She told him that Janice had told her what had happened, and she just thought he might want some company. Like anyone else suffering from traumatic news, Dr. Menken went through the details of the case with his colleague and ended by saying, "This came out of the blue. She didn't tell me she was suicidal. I even asked her about it 2 weeks ago, and she completely denied it. I don't know how I could have stopped it." His female colleague listened sympathetically, and said, "You couldn't have stopped it. Only the patient could. There are two ways you know if someone is suicidal—they either tell you they are, or they behave in a suicidal way. She did neither. You can't read minds." A silence ensued, and Dr. Menken felt tears coming to his eyes. He felt that his colleague understood him and that in some way she was absolving him. He said a simple "thank you" and explained that he needed to collect himself before he went home.

Dr. Menken continued to obsess about the circumstances of the suicide and what he might have done differently, but he knew he had a sympathetic ear down the hall if he needed one. In the future, if colleagues of his had the unfortunate development in their work of losing a patient to suicide, he knew what to do. He remembered that autumn afternoon when someone reached out to him, and he made it a point to reach out to others to pass on that kind of empathy and professionalism in helping colleagues in distress.

Stigma and Psychiatry

Special challenges emerge in the psychiatrist's career. One relates to the inevitable stigma attached to psychiatry as a discipline. Patients are stigmatized in the media as "homicidal maniacs" or "psychotic killers" or "narcissistic parasites" (Hyler et al. 1991). Psychiatrists themselves are often regarded as "not real doctors" and as ineffectual practitioners who cannot really do much for their patients.

Sadly, in everyday practice, doctors from throughout medicine often make jokes in the corridors of the hospital and at medical meetings about psychiatrists, and psychiatric residents are watching to see how their mentors and senior colleagues react to the barbs. Can they laugh it off, or do they react with a defensiveness that makes matters worse? In some cases they see colleagues who have taken on the contempt with which other specialists treat them as a burden they must carry. They have a form of self-loathing about what they do and how effective they are. This self-loathing can be internalized by trainees in the same way that virtuous aspects of one's professional role can be influential. If an attending on rounds in consultation-liaison settings acts apologetic about his or her knowledge to another specialist, there may be a transmission of this effect to the next generation of psychiatrists.

Negative images may be conveyed by the demeanor of the psychiatrist or even the way he or she dresses. A hurried bedside assessment of a patient in the intensive care unit or on a transplant service may convey a mixture of indifference and a lack of confidence in what help one can offer. Overly casual dress and lack of attention to one's appearance can convey a similar message about one's professional identity and one's value as a colleague to cynical colleagues in the hospital.

Learning by Observing

Individuals who decide to become psychiatrists are, by their very nature, observers. When we interview a patient, we listen for the "music" as well as the words. We study the turn of a lip, the flash of a smile, or the raising of an eyebrow. We listen not only for what is said but also for what goes unsaid in a life narrative and note the fluctuations in a patient's voice when a difficult subject emerges.

These skills serve us as psychiatrists well. We cannot be shut off when observing faculty, colleagues, or allied health professionals. Throughout training, the future psychiatrist takes in images of interactions, conflicts, grief, laughter, snippets of dialogue, and models of behavior in difficult situations. These experiences become a storehouse of examples of what a psychiatrist is and does.

Each of us assesses these images and classifies them according to the impression they make. Over time we assemble them into composites of those with whom we wish to identify and those from whom we wish to distance ourselves. We wish to be treated with respect and professionalism, so we look for models who treat others as we ourselves would like to be treated.

In other words, the hidden curriculum involves learning professionalism from observation in the same way we learn psychiatric diagnoses from observing our patients. The way we want others to experience us is the cornerstone of professionalism.

Key Points

- "Pimping" is a form of teaching that extends from long-standing tradition in medical education in which an attending physician shames a resident physician or medical student by posing questions in a manner that exposes the trainee's lack of knowledge.

- Professionalism or the lack of it is often learned from an informal or "hidden curriculum" where residents and medical students model the positive or negative behavior of their supervisors.

- The behavior of supervisors is inevitably internalized consciously or unconsciously by trainees.

- Evidence suggests that early-career physicians do not always recognize that they are engaging in unprofessional misconduct.

- Work-related stresses and depression decrease job satisfaction and thereby increase vulnerability to unprofessional behavior.

- Early career physicians must manage certain ethical tensions: assuming a new identity; integrating dual roles of learner and caregiver; navigating roles of physician and supervisor; and blending roles of learner and employee.

- The cornerstone of professionalism is the way we want others to experience us.

Chapter 10

Challenges Inherent in Teaching and Evaluating Professionalism

As efforts to characterize professionalism have become more central to medical education, extensive work has been performed to address the complexities of trying to teach and assess professionalism (Stern 2006; Wear and Aultman 2006), particularly when the definition itself is controversial. As the basis for evaluating professionalism, Arnold and Stern (2006) offered the following definition: *"Professionalism* is demonstrated through a foundation of clinical competence, communication skills, and ethical and legal understanding, upon which is built the aspiration to and wise application of the principles of professionalism: excellence, humanism, accountability, and altruism" (p. 19).

Arnold and Stern stressed that skills and knowledge are necessary but not sufficient to be professional in one's behavior, and certain personal qualities of "character" are essential. They also argued that this definition of professionalism offers a bridge to medical ethics. Specifically, they regarded ethics as a discipline that emphasizes issues of autonomy, justice, beneficence, and nonmaleficence, following the lead of Pellegrino and Thomasma (1981). They also included communication skills as foundational, because professional behavior is enacted through effective communication.

Definitions like the one proposed by Arnold and Stern are useful because of their comprehensiveness. However, they also lend themselves to critiques because of their potential to overlook subgroups of professionals and to understate the complexity of professional behavior.

In subsequent work, Reed et al. (2008) sought to characterize empirically the behaviors of "highly professional resident physicians." The authors used observations of first-year internal medicine residents at the Mayo Clinic over a 3-year period, looking at activities of special importance in postgraduate training, including effectiveness, timeliness, and completeness of patient-care tasks (e.g., performance of histories and physicals, "sign-outs," cross-coverage); effectiveness in communication with families; helpfulness in completion of tasks; level of integrity; commitment to one's own education; humanistic qualities; demonstration of empathy; and respectful interactions with others. This study revealed that residents with professionalism scores in the top 20% had higher scores on in-training knowledge/cognitive and clinical skill performance examinations. (There was no apparent correlation with conference attendance and scoring most highly on the scales of professional behavior.) This study, like some others, used an approach that looked at assessing professionalism in a manner that derived from and was attuned to the everyday work of a physician in training, rather than being organized through an *a priori* and perhaps less immediately meaningful conceptual framework of professionalism.

Castellani and Hafferty (2006), using social complexity theory as a way of analyzing professionalism, noted that the discourse on professionalism often has a totalizing or "one size fits all" quality to it, while neglecting other ways of practicing medical professionalism that may not fit neatly under the broad definitions. In particular, they noted that lifestyle and personal morality play key roles in the professional behavior of residents and medical students. In addition, the entrepreneurial spirit of many practicing physicians may also influence models of professionalism.

Regarding the impact of lifestyle and personal morality on professionalism, these authors stressed that broad changes have occurred in medicine in recent years. For example, women with children and/or other family responsibilities constitute a substantial segment of the physician workforce. Also, many early career physicians, just coming out of medical schools and residencies, are committed to balancing family time and their responsibilities to patients. These "newly minted" professionals may not accept the value system of dedication to work, to the exclusion of personal and family life, that has been seen as fundamental to the identity of the physician for decades (Myers and Gabbard 2008). From their perspective, the balance between family and work is itself a key precept of professionalism and may reflect a new construction of the view of personal and professional "boundaries." As we noted in Chapter 5, self-care is a critically important part of professionalism that exists in a dialectical relationship with altruism.

Beyond this "lifestyle professionalism," attitudes toward the economic aspects of clinical practice and professionalism have changed. Physicians have to pay their overhead expenses and make a living. With 47 million Americans unable to obtain health insurance, many physicians are wary of treating anyone who comes in the door. Whether one views this as economic viability or a more robust sense of entrepreneurialism, principles of business have arrived at the center of professionalism. Some (Castellani and Hafferty 2006) would argue that the patient's capacity to pay and the setting of healthcare delivery are factors that cannot be ignored.

Castellani and Hafferty (2006) emphasized that lifestyle professionalism and entrepreneurial professionalism are simply two of as many as seven competing clusters of professionalism. They cautioned that there is a risk of oversimplifying the discourse on professionalism that is currently filling the pages of journals and echoing through the classrooms of academia. The individual and subgroup differences, as well as economic realities, must be taken into account to fully appreciate the complexity of professional behavior.

The foregoing discussion of the complexities of defining the essence of professionalism is a good introduction to the challenges encountered when trying to develop a curriculum to teach psychiatric residents and psychiatrists who have been out in practice for awhile. One does not want to teach that conformity to a standard set of values and behaviors is mandated—that is, we do not want to create an army of robotic "Stepford psychiatrists." Nor do we want to produce one more set of perfectionistic behaviors for highly conscientious young physicians to obsess about achieving. Furthermore, we do not want to overvalue what can be learned from reading books and papers or sitting in a classroom. As we discussed in Chapter 9, the hidden curriculum is perhaps the most powerful force for all physicians in learning professional values and behaviors. In other words, professionalism is largely learned by observation and internalization of teachers, senior residents, and other role models. All physicians can undoubtedly recollect an attending that made them want to be a better physician by emulating what the role model did with patients. Similarly, all of us remember our disillusionment with well-known attending physicians who were insensitive and contemptuous human beings and who shaped us by serving as negative role models from whom we vowed to dissociate ourselves.

So how do we translate what we learn in the hidden curriculum into seminars, readings, and teaching in the classroom? The majority of the literature on professionalism is geared toward medical students (Duff 2004; Gaiser 2009; Klein et al. 2003; Stern 2006). There is little to guide the classroom instructor or the educator attempting to develop a didactic curriculum for psychiatric residents or for postgraduate physicians. In this final chapter we consider both curricula and evaluation methods, first for psychiatric residents and then for psychiatrists who have been out of residency training for a period of time.

Teaching and Evaluating Psychiatric Residents

Curriculum

In 1997, the Accreditation Council for Graduate Medical Education (ACGME) defined *professionalism* as a commitment to executing professional responsibilities, sensitivity to a diverse patient population, and adherence to ethical principles. ACGME identified six core competency areas in which resident physicians should gain proficiency. Schwartz et al. (2009) summarized these areas as six key attributes:

1. Altruism
2. Accountability
3. Excellence
4. Duty
5. Honor and integrity
6. Respect for others

Competency in professionalism will be established, according to the ACGME (Andrews and Burruss 2004, p. 59), by the resident's ability to

- Demonstrate respect, compassion, and integrity; a responsiveness to the needs of patients and society that supercedes self-interest; accountability to patients, society, and the profession; and a commitment to excellence and ongoing professional development.
- Demonstrate a commitment to ethical principles pertaining to provision or withholding of clinical care, confidentiality of patient information, informed consent, and business practices.
- Demonstrate sensitivity and responsiveness to patients' culture, age, gender, and disabilities.

In an effort to adapt these principles to psychiatry-specific activities, the American Association of Directors of Psychiatric Residency Training assembled a group of experienced educators, including Beresin, Davis, Herman, and Russell, who were charged with operationalizing these principles. They suggested that the following behaviors could be taught and evaluated as part of learning professionalism (Andrews and Burruss 2004, p. 59):

1. The resident shall demonstrate responsibility for his or her patient's care. This responsibility includes
   - Responding to patients' communications
   - Using the medical record for appropriate documentation of the course of illness and its treatment, providing coverage if unavailable, and coordinating care with other members of the medical and/or multidisciplinary team.
   - Providing for appropriate transfer or referral if necessary.
2. The resident will respond to communication from patients and health professionals in a timely manner. If unavailable, the resident will establish and communicate backup arrangements. The resident communicates clearly to patients and families about how to seek emergent and urgent care when necessary.
3. The resident shall demonstrate ethical behavior, as defined in the American Psychiatric Association's *Principles of Medical Ethics with Annotations Especially Applicable to Psychiatry.*
4. The resident shall demonstrate respect for culturally diverse patients and colleagues as persons, including their cultural identity (as influenced by age, gender, race, ethnicity, socioeconomic status, religion/spirituality, sexual orientation, country of origin, acculturation, language, and disabilities, among other factors).
5. The resident ensures continuity of care for patients and when it is appropriate to terminate care, does so appropriately and does not "abandon" patients.

Having identified these helpful precepts, the educator is still challenged by developing a classroom curriculum that pales in importance
compared with the hidden curriculum that psychiatric residents witness
each day in the clinical assignments. Nevertheless, a conceptual foundation must be laid for residents to assist them in their clinical work. Although each residency training program can organize the material as it
wishes, we suggest that the key components that need to be covered in
the context of a didactic curriculum for psychiatric residents include the
following:

1. *Ethics.* The teaching of ethics is most effective when the principles are
   learned through real clinical examples of ethical dilemmas that can be
   brought into the classroom.
2. *Professional boundaries and boundary violations.* The conceptual differences
   between boundary violations and boundary crossings (Gutheil and
   Gabbard 1993) should be taught, as well as the range of boundary issues
   encountered in psychiatric practice: confidentiality, place and space,
   language, dress, dual relationships, money, sexual contact (both during
   treatment and after), professional role, time and length of sessions.
3. *Multicultural sensitivity.* All residents should be taught how gender, race/
   ethnicity, religion, culture, and sexual orientation affect the clinical setting. The practice of cultural empathy can be discussed and demonstrated
   using case examples.
4. *Communication.* Although skills at communicating with patients may be
   taught in medical school, the psychiatric resident needs to go beyond that
   level to learn how to build a therapeutic alliance, the limits of useful self-
   disclosure, the focus on the patient's needs rather than his or her own,
   and how and when to communicate both transference and countertransference in the discourse of a session with a patient. The resident must
   also learn when and how to communicate with family members while
   preserving confidentiality.
5. *The role of supervision and consultation.* All residents need to be trained
   to conceptualize what they do in the context of a triad of patient, clinician, and supervisor/consultant. The messages they need to learn are
   that they cannot solve all dilemmas on their own, we are all prone to
   self-deception, and they need to seek help early on before things de-
   teriorate into unethical compromises.
6. *The essentials of professional behavior.* In residency training, it should not
   be assumed that residents know what it means to be professional. In the

curriculum, they need to learn the skills of prompt response to patient communications, documentation that is accurate without being obsessionally overinclusive, provision of coverage when the clinician is unavailable, working within a multidisciplinary team, transferring a patient or ending treatment in a professional manner, and involving families in an ethical way.

7. *Implications of the Internet.* Residents must be taught the basics of social networking sites, blogging, E-mail communication, and the risks inherent in all of these media. They must learn that professionalism is now broadly defined as including a compact with society as well as the individual patient, and that when contemplating what they will place on Facebook or other Internet sites they must remember that they are psychiatrists 24 hours a day and 7 days a week when they are in public settings.

8. *The increasing complexity of healthcare systems.* Residents need to be taught how to interface with third-party payers, managed care companies, and Medicare/Medicaid.

The goal of professionalism didactics, in conjunction with behaviors modeled to residents, is to instill a *way of thinking* about why a behavior is considered unethical or unprofessional. Residents must develop an understanding and internalization of what is behind the code of professional behavior. To facilitate this process, various teaching techniques can be used to enhance learning, including case discussions, role playing, and open sharing of opinions in an environment that is perceived as nonjudgmental and open to varied opinions. Individuals must have time for self-reflection, which is critical to integrating professionalism principles into their moral structure in a meaningful way, rather than just understanding "rules of professionalism" as though they are black and white.

As noted, the mantle of professionalism can be invoked to demand conformity to arbitrary standards in a destructive manner that discourages individual innovation and creativity. The misuses of professionalism must also be taught to residents in the didactic curriculum. For example, they need to avoid using the word "unprofessional" as an insult. The culture of "professionalism" can be used to marginalize and exclude those who think differently than we do. The very essence of psychiatry relies upon an understanding of and appreciation for individual characteristics—both of the patient and of the psychiatrist—that must allow for individual variation and flexibility in how we see ourselves and our colleagues. There are few inflexible rules regarding professional behaviors. Moreover, the sphere of transference and countertransference provides a rich network in which we operate and is unique to the field of psychiatry.

In a medical and psychiatric culture in which professionalism is taught as an ethical and central value, calling someone "unprofessional" can be riddled with contempt and degradation in much the same manner as a racial epithet or a four-letter word. It can have serious and longstanding personal and professional consequences. Consider the following example.

> Dr. Phillips was a third-year resident in her psychiatric training and was increasing in her professional competence and her feelings of self-confidence as she moved forward in her education. She had always received feedback that she collaborated positively on teams, that she had excellent clinical skills with her patients, and that she was diligent regarding her call responsibilities. Her mother fell ill with cancer, and she began to take trips to visit her and help her make medical decisions about her care. At times, she appeared worried and distracted on rounds, particularly when she had just learned of her mother's illness. There was a 6-month period in which she scheduled several trips out of town due to problems with the chemotherapy, recurrent life-threatening infections, and her mother's eventual death. She worked to secure clinical coverage for those times she was away but did not always receive support from her colleagues as they became frustrated at being asked to take repeated calls. The program had to step in to work through issues in arranging clinical coverage in a difficult situation. In the meeting to work through these issues, it was suggested by both her co-residents and her faculty that she was "unprofessional" in her decisions to go home to see her family. The label stuck, and she heard "unprofessional" used at other times—on rounds if she did not know an answer and even months later when the situation had resolved. She began to fear meetings with the faculty, and it changed how she viewed herself, her colleagues, and how she felt about her training program.

In this case, a complicated, multifaceted situation involving tensions and complicated group dynamics became focused onto one person. Calling Dr. Phillips "unprofessional" enabled the group to projectively disavow their own shortcomings and deposit all of them into a convenient scapegoat. Dr. Phillips, who for painful personal reasons could not always be available, became the carrier of the group's conflicts regarding a variety of competing personal and professional interests and obligations inherent in a training program. Instead of attempting to work those through in a collegial and respectful way, they designated Dr. Phillips as "unprofessional." It was certainly difficult for Dr. Phillips to manage a situation with the illness and loss of her mother in another city. It was a challenge for her colleagues and faculty to cover for her. These difficulties could have been discussed constructively.

Much like the vicissitudes of political correctness, professionalism can be a pendulum that swings to and fro over time. We hold a high standard and may at times lose sight of realistic expectations for ourselves and our colleagues. The pendulum of professionalism can swing too far in the direction of perfection. Moreover, professionalism does not always mean that two people will have exactly the same clinical judgment. Sometimes in a disagreement we fall back on criticizing someone else's professionalism and, ironically, we behave in a manner that is itself lacking in professionalism.

The label of "unprofessional" can also be used in a slippery way by someone who is angling to get out of difficult situations.

> Dr. Benton was the supervisor for Dr. Thomas in an outpatient clinic. Dr. Benton had some concerns about Dr. Thomas's prescribing practices and told him so formally in his annual evaluation. Dr. Thomas refuted these concerns, simultaneously going to the management and telling them that Dr. Benton was unprofessional. He made allegations that Dr. Benton used unprofessional humor with colleagues and staff in the workplace and joked inappropriately. At this point, the real concerns about Dr. Thomas's prescribing became lost in larger discussions about Dr. Benton's behavior, which none of the colleagues or staff had experienced as inappropriate. In this situation, Dr. Benton's concerns were justified, and Dr. Thomas was trying to shift attention away from himself and onto Dr. Benton with allegations about "unprofessional" behavior, with accusations that in this case were unwarranted.

One of the problems inherent in a medical culture in which professionalism is idealized, taught, and built into formalized educational programs and committees, is that it can be held over people's heads as if someone has it and someone else does not. It can become a tool of those in power versus those who are on the margins or lower in the academic or clinical hierarchy. As Lesser et al. (2010) clarified, professionalism is a systems issue, and we should be working toward the aspects of it that can be learned, taught, and negotiated in a system. One danger of calling people unprofessional without looking at the broader context of a situation is sounding holier than thou or talking down from a pedestal, the self-appointed adjudicator of what is professional and what is not.

Similarly, the implication in Dr. Thomas's allegation that the use of humor is a category of poor professionalism is highly questionable. It certainly can be when the humor is aggressive and designed to ridicule a co-worker, colleague, or patient. However, humor can help clinicians survive in highly stressful circumstances that test one's tolerance to its limits. Ventilating with members of a treatment team in private after a difficult patient has been seen in the emergency department is a common practice that forges a bond between team members and underscores the fact that "we all survived that impossible situation." One must be careful that humorous comments are not said in front of family members or patients. That said, there are many ways to incorporate humor into clinical meetings with patients and families that may serve a constructive purpose. Humor involves a process of stepping back from a situation and reflecting on it in such a way that one has new insights about it that may be genuinely funny. The key in these situations is to assure that one is laughing *with* the patient and not *at* the patient. As with boundaries, context is everything in the use of humor, and there is an inevitable trial and error process when one tests out to what extent a patient can make use of humor. In any case, we do not want to mindlessly designate the use of humor as an unprofessional practice and consign us all to a sober and dull professional existence.

Evaluation

Professionalism has traditionally been conceptualized as involving innate characteristics that professionals possess that have been deemed virtuous based on cultural norms and standards (Lesser et al. 2010). This limited perspective of professionalism poses a dilemma for the practice of medicine and psychiatry. It creates a barrier for the implementation of standardized measures of assessing competence in the area of professionalism. Moreover, if professionalism is limited to core values that precede medical training or the practice of medicine, it would be tempting to fail to hold medical professionals accountable for certain unethical or unprofessional behavior. It could potentially negate the utility of didactic curriculums in training programs that serve to teach and promote professional behavior. Lack of this type of training in residency programs could have a negative long-term impact on the healthcare system as a whole.

   Professionalism skills go beyond character to teachable behaviors. Lesser et al. (2010) proposed that the outlook of professionalism should evolve to sophisticated competencies that can and must be taught and refined over a lifetime of practice. This notion provides opportunity for constant reevaluation and growth of professional standards for medical students, residents, and even attending physicians. Professionalism problems in residency forecast trouble later in the career of physicians (van Mook et al. 2010). These risk prognosticators provide much credence to the need for a didactic curriculum and measures for assessing competence in the field of medicine.

The six core competency areas noted at the beginning of this chapter encompass many attitudes and behavioral characteristics of professionals, and these can serve as a way of organizing the assessment or evaluation process. *Altruism* is defined as the commitment to always act in the best interests of the patient. This measure can be operationalized by observing a value system in which the resident places the patient's interests over his or her own interest. Obviously, such emphasis of the patient's needs over one's own resides on a continuum, and one can compromise one's professionalism if self-care is completely neglected. *Accountability* is demonstrated by being consistent and reliable to patients and colleagues. Are phone calls, pages, and e-mails answered promptly? Is the resident available in times of natural disasters or public health crises? Does the resident follow up on patient care issues (i.e., results of imaging studies) or educational pursuits (i.e., attendance at academic rounds)? Punctuality with patients and with colleagues can also be measured.

Excellence as it relates to professionalism refers to making a conscientious effort to exceed ordinary expectations and to demonstrate a commitment to the pursuit of learning what one does not know. This dimension also entails recognizing limitations in knowledge, skill, or areas of expertise. Excellence is *not* the same as perfection. Physicians are therefore expected to know when it is appropriate to refer patients to a specialist for consultation or when to seek supervision for difficult cases. *Duty* is another core competency that involves displaying a commitment to service. It transcends being available and responsive to the needs of the patients and leads one to advocate for the best care of patients and even volunteering one's skills and expertise for the welfare of the community. Failing to document or to collect collateral information regarding a patient to maximize care would be an example of a deficiency in the execution of duty.

Honor and integrity refer to honesty and the adherence of ethical and moral standards as it relates to patient care and interactions with colleagues. These principles also include being mindful of and avoiding conflicts of interest with patient care. This competency area is often put to the test in evaluating acceptable standards for receiving gifts from pharmaceutical sales representatives and how one manages professional boundaries with patients. *Respect for others* is closely affiliated with honor and integrity. It involves interacting with patients, colleagues, and support/ancillary staff in a manner that is respectful. Does the resident talk about patients or colleagues in a denigrating way? Does the resident use pejorative terms to describe patients' behavior, appearance, ethnic background, or disease states? A simple measure of respect is the refusal to take phone calls during patient encounters in order to emphasize that the patient's time in treatment is held in high regard (Schwartz et al. 2009).

Having outlined what is being measured, we now turn to some tools that may be used to assess for competency in professionalism. Resident evaluation forms can provide global ratings from supervisors but often lack sufficient specificity. Inherent in these measures are the potential for subjectivity, delays in receiving feedback, and poor clarification of specific areas that are in need of improvement.

So-called 360-degree evaluations have become highly valued in providing feedback on professionalism. Although they became popular as a way of dealing with disruptive physicians, they have now been used more generally both for residents and for attending physicians. In brief, those who work with the resident are asked to fill out checklists periodically that provide specific feedback about desired and undesirable behaviors. The great advantage of this form of assessment is that the feedback comes from individuals with different backgrounds (i.e., nurses, colleagues, ancillary staff, patients, and supervisors) and provides specific data regarding strengths and weaknesses. This method is probably most valuable for highlighting areas in need of improvement. One of the drawbacks is that there is a greater vulnerability to rater or sampling bias. It is possible that the physician may be rated poorly because of personal attitudes toward the physician that might not accurately reflect skill set in each competency domain. Hence this measure requires a large number of evaluators to be considered a reliable measure of performance. Another obstacle to persuading coworkers to fill out the forms is fear of retaliation by the person being rated. If the evaluations do not preserve the evaluator's anonymity, there is an increased likelihood that the evaluator may not be completely honest.

Verbal feedback from supervision through direct observation behind a one-way mirror, through video or audio recordings, or through reporting of process notes in supervision is another standard source of assessment. This method provides a consistent analysis of progression of skills. The results could be skewed due to potential for the residents to be on their best behavior or to replay the therapeutic encounter in a manner that portrays them in a positive light.

Chart review can be a useful means of evaluating one's accountability and duty. It is inexpensive and targets specific criteria for meeting certain standards. Checklists for specific criteria, however, may not adequately reflect the content of information being transmitted.

Formal evaluation sessions with a training director allow for evaluators to discuss areas of concern that they may hesitate to document in an effort to avoid tainting an academic record. Interventions can be implemented to address professional issues that are discussed. The resident can also receive clarification on areas of miscommunication and may ask questions to help facilitate improvement. The disadvantage of this measure is that evaluators may not be as forthright due to fear of conflict and/or intense emotional reactions from the person who is being evaluated.

Just as the respect of individuality and creativity is important in curricula, the need to take flexibility and individual variation into account is equally important in assessment of residents. During psychiatric training, the learner is introduced to the dynamics of interpersonal interaction and develops an appreciation for the fluidity of each patient encounter. Evaluators must avoid making unwarranted generalizations or stereotypes about professional behavior while remaining sensitive to the irreducible truth that there are unique learning styles and unique professional identities that do not lend themselves to facile measurement. As we have argued throughout this book, professionalism is not a formulaic value system that an educator can teach from a lesson plan and evaluate from a brief quiz. It is a body of knowledge that requires critical thinking and skill building techniques that evolve during the course of one's career (Lesser et al. 2010).

> Dr. Clark has been treating Mrs. Canton, an 87-year-old woman with depression, for 2 years. During the course of her twice-weekly psychotherapy treatment, Mrs. Canton developed metastatic cancer and became too physically weak to attend her psychotherapy appointments. Dr. Clark then met with her at her bedside in a long-term care facility and continued the therapy in an attempt to address Mrs. Canton's worsening depressed mood and help her deal with terrifying end-of-life issues. During some of the sessions Dr. Clark held Mrs. Canton's hand to comfort her during the therapy.

A rigid evaluation of this approach might conclude that Dr. Clark is violating the frame of therapy and professional boundaries by conducting therapy in an environment where staff walk in and out of the room and by holding her hand instead of observing the standard boundary of no physical contact with the patient. In assessing the professionalism of this treatment, the supervisor must take the context into account and determine if Dr. Clark is in any way exploiting the patient or hurting the treatment. Is she actually demonstrating compassion and attempting to avoid abandoning her ailing patient during her imminent death? This case example serves as a reminder that boundaries must be flexible, and professionalism can expand with the boundaries in such situations. One skill to be acquired by residents is to think critically about each interaction according to the risks and benefits of a treatment decision.

As noted in Chapter 1, one of the unique features of psychiatry is its emphasis on countertransference as a source of useful information. In assessing residents, supervisors must assess how the resident manages such feelings—do the feelings result in unprofessional behaviors or do they lead to productive thinking about the process of treatment? When a resident has the courage to say "I can't stand this patient" or "I feel attracted to this patient," the supervisor must assess if the resident can collaborate with the supervisor to investigate what those countertransference feelings say about the patient and the therapist as well as what they say about the state of the therapy process. Supervisors, of course, play a key role in creating an atmosphere in which these feelings can be brought out into the open. Instead of helping the supervisee learn to deal with strong feelings in clinical encounters, some supervisors will shame and humiliate the budding therapist for having such feelings. The evaluation of the young therapist's professionalism does not hinge on whether such feelings are present but on how they are handled both in the supervisory process and in the psychotherapy.

Teaching and Evaluating Practicing Psychiatrists

As the foregoing discussion of the abuse of power in the supervisory relationship suggests, it is imperative to educate senior colleagues about the impact they have on trainees as part of a professionalism curriculum (Gaiser 2009; Markakis et al. 2000). In essence the goal is to create an entire social environment that is sensitive to and supportive of professional behavior and ethical principles imperative to the practice of psychiatry, and more specifically, the training and practice of psychiatrists. The role of professionalism and professional boundaries in psychiatric practice is a relatively recent development in psychiatric education, and generations of psychiatrists in practice acknowledge that they had no education about such matters when they went through training.

Just as professionalism has become a core competency for residents, physicians pursuing maintenance of certification also must demonstrate competency in professionalism. In the current setting, such education is generally gained through continuing medical education of one kind or another. For the most part, such education is based on self-assessment (American Board of Medical Specialties 2010). Unfortunately, breaches in professional behavior by physicians have largely been addressed in a retroactive, reactive manner rather than through an educational and preventive model. This is seen in the recent Joint Commission Leadership Standards that mandate hospital leaders to create and implement ways of managing disruptive and inappropriate behaviors (The Joint Commission 2008).

Because education in professionalism now is required to begin in medical school and continue into lifelong learning endeavors, it is necessary to take on a preventive model approach in hopes that incidents of unprofessional behavior will decrease throughout the field of medicine. In light of the fact that there are a large number of well-established psychiatrists in the community and in academic centers who have had little to no formal training in professionalism, it has become necessary to develop continuing medical education curricula and present the material in a manner that is both meaningful and influential to both novice and experienced physicians.

Although much of the teaching to this more experienced population can parallel what is taught to residents, developing and delivering effective teaching on professionalism to practicing psychiatrists has a unique set of challenges associated with it. For example, the business or entrepreneurial aspects of practice referred to by Castellani and Hafferty (2006) may be of much greater concern to established clinicians than it is to psychiatric residents. Those who organize continuing education presentations must take into account that the members of the audience are concerned about making a living, and professionalism principles must be placed in a context that is reasonable from an economic perspective. Similarly, the challenges posed by healthcare systems and third-party payers must be addressed to make the content of presentations more relevant to the learners.

In addition, many seasoned clinicians will regard such education with contempt and will argue that they already know everything they need to know about professionalism. They can easily feel that the educator is talking down to them. Hence another challenge revolves around the method of learning. Some studies show that both residents and seasoned clinicians (Bower et al. 2008; Klein et al. 2003) report a preference for passive didactic learning, but professionalism concepts do not easily lend themselves to this model.

McLaren et al. (2011) discussed some techniques that they have found useful to educate advanced clinicians about professionalism. The most formidable obstacle is to overcome the defensive posture of the learners. They often feel that the teachers are accusing them of being unprofessional by virtue of being told they need education in this area. Clinical vignettes involving other physicians can be used so that they feel less threatened. Then the psychiatrist-learners can be active participants in discussing what aspects of the colleague's behavior need to be addressed as unprofessional. In addition, an audience response system can be used in which the participants electronically submit answers to multiple-choice questions anonymously. If someone's answer is an outlier, no one but that person knows, and those who are outliers end up receiving feedback from colleagues by the mere fact of the disparity between their answer and those of others. This disparity may actually result in some internal questioning and reflection.

As discussed earlier regarding teaching professionalism to residents, it is essential for residents to have time for reflection to incorporate new professional concepts into the moral framework of the individual (Gaiser 2009). Using clinical vignettes that are subtle, rather than clear cut "bad" versus "good" behavior, allows those who are learning to identify with the physician in the vignette. Moreover, this identification is nonthreatening because the scenarios are more representative of "real-world" complexities they confront in their actual practice (McLaren et al. 2011). It also allows them to see some of their own flaws and to be open to seeing both their strengths and weaknesses rather than seeing physicians with professionalism problems as all good or all bad.

Assessing senior psychiatrists for the time being must be relegated to hospital committees or peer review procedures when there is a complaint. It is extremely difficult to implement 360-degree evaluations for practicing psychiatrists in the current climate of practice. However, hospitals have quality assurance committees that review documentation and other procedures in inpatient units. Some assessment of professionalism is being done as a byproduct of such reviews. As we stated in Chapter 8, there is also an inherent obligation that we all have to give feedback to someone who is behaving unprofessionally and inform the colleague of ways to receive help, even when that feedback is unwelcome. Being our "brother's keeper" is inherent in professionalism.

A discussion of teaching and evaluation of professionalism must, of course, end with a caveat. No psychiatric resident or psychiatrist can be under continuous scrutiny. Professionalism ultimately comes down to the way we behave when *no one* is watching or listening except our patients. In the final analysis, they may be our most consistent evaluators. Every good clinician knows that our patients are continually "supervising" us, and it is wise to listen to what they say about us either directly or "between the lines."

Key Points

- The perspective of professionalism has traditionally been linked to demonstrating good moral values and standards.

- The traditional neglect of professionalism in training may limit physicians' accountability for competency in this area.

- Didactic curriculums in training programs have served to teach and promote professional behavior.

- The ACGME has identified six core competency areas of professionalism for resident physicians: altruism, accountability, excellence, duty, honor and integrity, and respect for others.

- The idea of professionalism can be misused when calling people "unprofessional," and because this term weighs heavily it should be used with caution and care.

- Several evaluation measures are available to assess for competency for psychiatric residents.

- Senior psychiatrists may react defensively at the prospect of being taught and evaluated, but there are techniques to make such programs more palatable.

References

Adebimpe VR: Overview: white norms and psychiatric diagnosis of black patients. Am J Psychiatry 138:279–285, 1981

Ahmer S, Yousafzai A, Siddiqi M, et al: Bullying of trainee psychiatrists in Pakistan: a cross-sectional questionnaire survey. Acad Psychiatry 33:335–339, 2009

Allen JG, Fonagy P, Bateman A: Mentalizing in Clinical Practice. Washington, DC, American Psychiatric Publishing, 2008

American Association of Medical Colleges: Executive Summary of the AAMC Annual Development Survey. Washington, DC, American Association of Medical Colleges, 2009

American Board of Internal Medicine Foundation, American Board of Internal Medicine, American College of Physicians-American Society of Internal Medicine, et al: Medical professionalism in the new millennium: the physician charter. Ann Intern Med 136:243–246, 2002

American Board of Medical Specialties: Maintenance of Certification Competencies and Criteria. Chicago, IL, American Board of Medical Specialties. Available at: http://www.abms.org/Maintenance_of_Certification/MOC_competencies.aspx. Accessed November 5, 2010.

American Medical Association: Principles of Medical Ethics. Chicago, IL, American Medical Association, 2001. Available at: http://www.ama-assn.org/ama/pub/physician-resources/medical-ethics/code-medical-ethics/principles-medical-ethics.page? Accessed July 8, 2011.

American Medical Association: Guidelines for Physician-Patient Electronic Communications. Chicago, IL, American Medical Association, 2005. Available at http://www.ama-assn.org/ama/pub/about-ama/our-people/member-groups-sections/young-physicians-section/advocacy-resources/guidelines-physician-patient-electronic-communications.page. Accessed 2010.

American Psychiatric Association: Commission on Psychotherapy by Psychiatrists (COPP): position statement on therapies focused on attempts to change sexual orientation (reparative or conversion therapies). Am J Psychiatry 157:1719–1721, 2000

American Psychiatric Association: The Principles of Medical Ethics With Annotations Especially Applicable to Psychiatry. Washington, DC, American Psychiatric Association, 2001

Andrews L, Burruss J: Core Competencies for Psychiatric Education: Defining, Teaching, and Assessing Resident Competence. Washington, DC, American Psychiatric Publishing, 2004

Arnold L, Stern DT: What is medical professionalism?, in Measuring Medical Professionalism. Edited by Stern DT. Oxford, UK, Oxford University Press, 2006, pp 15–37

Beauchamp TL: The philosophical basis of psychiatric ethics, in Psychiatric Ethics. Edited by Bloch S, Green SA. New York, Oxford University Press, 2009, pp 25–48

Beauchamp TL, Childress JF: Principles of Biomedical Ethics, 5th Edition. New York, Oxford University Press, 2001

Bell CC, Mehta H: The misdiagnosis of black patients with manic depressive illness. J Natl Med Assoc 74:1464–1480, 1998

Bower EA, Girard DE, Wessel K, et al: Barriers to innovation in continuing medical education. J Contin Educ Health Prof 28:148–156, 2008

Bradshaw W: The Coffee-Pot Affair: an episode in the life of a therapeutic community. Hosp Community Psychiatry 23:33–38, 1972

Brenner C: The Mind in Conflict. New York, International Universities Press, 1982

Brewer B: Primary care has rewards despite hassles. The Wall Street Journal Online. June 3, 2008. Available at: http://online.wsj.com/article/SB121252805133942701.html. Accessed 2008.

Brown L (ed): The New Shorter Oxford English Dictionary, Vol. 2. New York, Oxford University Press, 1993

Campbell EG, Regan S, Gruen RL, et al: Professionalism in medicine: results of a national survey of physicians. Ann Intern Med 147:795–802, 2007

Castellani B, Hafferty FW: The complexities of medical professionalism: a preliminary investigation, in Professionalism in Medicine: Critical Perspectives. Edited by Wear D, Aultman JN. New York, Springer, 2006, pp 1–23

Celenza A: The threat of male-to-female erotic transference. J Am Psychoanal Assoc 54:1207–1231, 2006

Chretien KC, Greysen SR, Chretien JP, et al: On-line posting of unprofessional content by medical students. JAMA 302:1309–1315, 2009

Clinton BK, Silverman BC, Brendel DH: Patient-targeted Googling: the ethics of searching on line for patient information. Harv Rev Psychiatry 18:103–112, 2010

Coleman D, Baker FM: Misdiagnosis of schizophrenia among older black veterans. J Nerv Ment Dis 182:527–528, 1994

Council on Ethical and Judicial Affairs: Code of Medical Ethics. Chicago, IL, American Medical Association, 2002

Coverdale J, McCullough LB, Roberts LW: The ethics of psychiatric education. Psychiatr Clin North Am 32:413–421, 2009

Dawkins R: The Self Gene. New York, Oxford University Press, 1976

Detsky AS: The art of pimping. JAMA 301:1379–1381, 2009

Dorsey ER, Jarjajoura D, Rutecki GW: The influence of controllable lifestyle on recent trends in specialty choice by US medical students. JAMA 290:1173–1178, 2003

Drane JF: Competency to give an informed consent: a model for making clinical assessments. JAMA 252:925–927, 1984

Drescher J: I'm your handyman: a history of reparative therapies. J Homosex 36:19–42, 1998

Duff P: Teaching and assessing professionalism in medicine. Obstet Gynecol 104:1362–1366, 2004

Dunn LB, Green Hammond K, Roberts LW: Delaying care, avoiding stigma: residents' attitudes toward obtaining personal health care. Acad Med 84:242–250, 2009

Epstein RS, Simon RI, Kay GG: Assessing boundary violations in psychotherapy: survey results with the exploitation index. Bull Menninger Clin 56:150–166, 1992

Equal Employment Opportunity Commission. Title VII of the Civil Rights Act of 1964. Available at: http://www.eeoc.gov/laws/statutes/titlevii.cfm. Accessed February 2011.

Freidson E: Professionalism: The Third Logic. Chicago, IL, University of Chicago Press, 2001

Freud S: The taboo of virginity (contributions to the psychology of love III) (1918), in The Standard Edition of the Complete Psychological Works of Sigmund Freud, Volume 11. Translated and edited by Strachey J. London, Hogarth Press, 1957, pp 191–208

Freud S: Group psychology and the analysis of the ego (1921), in The Standard Edition of the Complete Psychological Works of Sigmund Freud, Vol 18. Translated and edited by Strachey J. London, Hogarth Press, 1955, pp 67–143

Gabbard GO: The exit line: heightened transference-countertransference manifestations at the end of the hour. J Am Psychoanal Assoc 30:579–598, 1982

Gabbard GO: The role of compulsiveness in the normal physician. JAMA 254:2926–2929, 1985

Gabbard GO: Splitting in hospital treatment. Am J Psychiatry 146:444–451, 1989

Gabbard GO: On hate in love relationships: the narcissism of minor differences revisited. Psychoanal Q 62:229–238, 1993

Gabbard GO: Treatment of borderline patients in a multiple-treater setting. Psychiatr Clin North Am 17:839–850, 1994

Gabbard GO: Countertransference: the emerging common ground. Int J Psychoanal 76:475–485, 1995

Gabbard GO: Lessons to be learned from the study of sexual boundary violations. Am J Psychother 50:311–322, 1996

Gabbard GO: Boundary violations, in Psychiatric Ethics, 3rd Edition. Edited by Bloch S, Chodoff P, Green SA. New York, Oxford University Press, 1999, pp 141–160

Gabbard GO: Disguise or consent: problems and recommendations concerning the publication and presentation of clinical material. Int J Psychoanal 81:1071–1086, 2000

Gabbard GO: Cyberpassion: E-rotic transference on the Internet. Psychoanal Q 70:719–737, 2001

Gabbard GO: Post-termination sexual boundary violations. Psychiatr Clin North Am 25:593–603, 2002

Gabbard GO: Psychodynamic Psychiatry in Clinical Practice, 4th Edition. Washington, DC, American Psychiatric Publishing, 2005

Gabbard GO: Professional boundaries in psychotherapy, in The American Psychiatric Publishing Textbook of Psychotherapeutic Treatments. Edited by Gabbard GO. Washington, DC, American Psychiatric Publishing, 2008, pp 809–827

Gabbard GO: Long-Term Psychodynamic Psychotherapy: A Basic Text, 2nd Edition. Washington, DC, American Psychiatric Publishing, 2010

Gabbard GO, Crisp-Han H: Teaching professional boundaries to psychiatric residents. Acad Psychiatry 34:369–372, 2010

Gabbard GO, Lester EP: Boundaries and Boundary Violations in Psychoanalysis. Washington, DC, American Psychiatric Publishing, 2003

Gabbard GO, Menninger RW: The psychology of postponement in the medical marriage. JAMA 261:2378–2381, 1989

Gabbard GO, Nadelson C: Professional boundaries in the physician-patient relationship. JAMA 273:1445–1449, 1995

Gabbard G, Kassaw K, Perez-Garcia G: Professional boundaries in the era of the Internet. Acad Psychiatry 35:168–174, 2011

Gaiser RR: The teaching of professionalism during residency: why it is failing and a suggestion to improve its success. Anesth Analg 108:948–954, 2009

Gaw AC: Culture, Ethnicity, and Mental Illness. Washington, DC, American Psychiatric Press, 1993

Gray F: The Tuskegee Syphilis Study: The Real Story and Beyond. Montgomery, AL, New South Books, 1998

Greenwald AG, McGhee DE, Schwartz JL: Measuring individual differences in implicit cognition: the implicit association test. J Pers Soc Psychol 74:1464–1480, 1998

Guseh JS 2nd, Brendel RW, Brendel DH: Medical professionalism in the age of online social networking. J Med Ethics 35:584–586, 2009

Gutheil TG, Gabbard GO: The concept of boundaries in clinical practice: theoretical and risk management dimensions. Am J Psychiatry 150:188–196, 1993

Harbaugh WT, Mayr U, Burghart DR: Neural responses to taxation and voluntary giving reveal motives for charitable donations. Science 316:1622–1625, 2007

Heru N, Gagne G, Strong D: Medical student mistreatment results in symptoms of posttraumatic stress. Acad Psychiatry 33:302–306, 2009

Hobday G, Mellman L, Gabbard GO: Clinical case conference: complex sexualized transferences when the patient is male and the therapist female. Am J Psychiatry 165:1525–1530, 2008

Hoop JG: Hidden ethical dilemmas in psychiatric residency training: the psychiatry resident as dual agent. Acad Psychiatry 28:183–189, 2004

Hundert EM: A model for ethical problem solving in medicine, with practical applications. Am J Psychiatry 144:839–846, 1987

Hyler SE, Gabbard GO, Schneider I: From homicidal maniacs to narcissistic parasites: stigmatization of the mentally ill in the movies. Hosp Community Psychiatry 42:1044–1048, 1991

Ingelfinger FJ: Arrogance. N Engl J Med 303:1507–1511, 1980

Institute of Medicine: Conflict of Interest in Medical Research, Education, and Practice. Washington, DC, National Academies Press, 2009

Inui T: A Flag in the Wind: Educating for Professionalism in Medicine. Washington, DC, Association of American Medical Colleges, 2003

Jain SH: Practicing medicine in the age of Facebook. N Engl J Med 361:649–651, 2009

Jain S, Hoop JG, Dunn LB, et al: Psychiatry residents' attitudes on ethics and professionalism: multisite survey results. Ethics Behav 20:10–20, 2010

Johnston S, Peacock M: Developing professionalism across the generations, in Teaching Medical Professionalism. Edited by Cruess RL, Cruess SR, Steinert Y. Cambridge, UK, Cambridge University Press, 2009

Jones BE, Gray BA, Parson EB: Manic-depressive illness among poor urban blacks. Am J Psychiatry 138:654–657, 1981

Jonsen AR, Siegler M, Winslade WJ: Clinical Ethics: A Practical Approach to Ethical Decisions in Clinical Medicine, 5th Edition. New York, McGraw-Hill/Appleton and Lange, 2002

Just how tainted has medicine become? (editorial) Lancet 359:1167, 2002

Kahn MW: Etiquette-based medicine. N Engl J Med 358:1988–1989, 2008

Kantrowitz JL: Writing About Patients: Responsibilities, Risks, and Ramifications. New York, Other Press, 2006

Kass LR: Professing ethically: on the place of ethics in defining medicine. JAMA 249:1305–1310, 1983

Kassaw K, Gabbard G: The ethics of E-mail communication in psychiatry. Psychiatr Clin North Am 25:666–674, 2002

Kelly E, Nisker J: Increasing bioethics education in preclinical medical curricula: what ethical dilemmas do clinical clerks experience? Acad Med 84:498–504, 2009

Kirch D: President's address, presented at American Association of Medical Colleges annual meeting, San Antonio, TX, November 2008. Available at: https://www.aamc.org/download/169724/data/kirchspeech2008.pdf. Accessed 2010.

Klein EJ, Jackson JC, Kratz L, et al: Teaching professionalism to residents. Acad Med 78:26–34, 2003

La Puma J, Stocking CB, La Voie D, et al: When physicians treat members of their own families. N Engl J Med 325:1290–1294, 1991

Lagu T, Kaufman EJ, Asch DA, et al: Content of weblogs written by health professionals. J Gen Intern Med 23:1642–1646, 2008

Lane LW: Residency ethics training in the United States: special considerations and early experience, in Symposium 1990 Proceedings of the Westminster Institute for Ethics and Human Values: Medical Ethics for Medical Students. London, Ontario, Canada, 1990, pp 21–32

Leary K: Racial enactments in dynamic treatment. Psychoanalytic Dialogues 10:639–653, 2000

Lesser CS, Lucey CR, Egener B, et al: A behavioral and systems view of professionalism. JAMA 304:2732–2737, 2010

Lewers ET: Guidelines of Patient-Physician Electronic Mail: Report to the Board of Trustees, American Medical Association. Chicago, IL, American Medical Association, 2000. Available at: http://www.ama-assn.org/meetings/public/annual00/reports/bot/bot2a00.rtf. Accessed December 26, 2001.

Linzer M, Visser MR, Oort FJ, et al: Predicting and preventing physician burnout: results from the United States and The Netherlands. Am J Med 111:170–175, 2001

Liss JL, Welner A, Robins E, et al: Psychiatric symptoms in white and black inpatients, I: record study. Compr Psychiatry 14:475–481, 1973

Louie A, Coverdale J, Roberts L: Balancing the personal and the professional: should and can we teach this? Acad Psychiatry 31:129–132, 2007

Markakis KM, Beckman HB, Suchman AL, et al: The path of professionalism: cultivating humanistic values and attitudes in residency training. Acad Med 75:141–149, 2000

McDaniel SH, Beckman HB, Morse DS, et al: Physician self-disclosure in primary care visits: enough about you, what about me? Arch Intern Med 167:1321–1326, 2007

McKegney CP: Medical education: a neglectful and abusive family system. Fam Med 21:452–457, 1989

McLaren K, Lord J, Murray S: Perspective: delivering effective and engaging continuing medical education on physicians' disruptive behavior. Acad Med 86:612–617, 2011

Meritor Savings Bank v. Vinson, 477 U.S. 57 (1986)

Mitchell S: Gender and sexual orientation in the age of postmodernism: the plight of the perplexed clinician. Gender and Psychoanalysis 1:45–74, 1996

Myers M, Gabbard GO: The Physician as Patient: A Clinical Handbook for Mental Health Professionals. Washington, DC, American Psychiatric Publishing, 2008

Nadelson CC: Ethics, empathy, and gender in health care. Am J Psychiatry 150:1309–1314, 1993

Nath C, Schmidt R, Gunel E: Perceptions of professionalism vary most with educational rank and age. J Dent Educ 70:825–834, 2006

Obama Addresses Physicians at AMA Meeting: Transcript of President Obama's Remarks. June 15, 2009. Chicago, IL, American Medical Association, 2009. Available at http://www.ama-assn.org/ama/pub/about-ama/our-people/house-delegates/2009-annual-meeting/speeches/president-obama-speech.shtml. Accessed 2011.

Painter NI: The History of White People. New York, WW Norton, 2010

Pellegrino ED, Thomasma DC: A Philosophical Basis of Medical Practice: Charter Philosophy and Ethic of the Healing Professions. New York, Oxford University Press, 1981

Petersdorf RG: Fraud, irresponsible authorship, and their causes: the pathogenesis of fraud in medical science. Ann Intern Med 104:252–254, 1986

Phillips SH, Richardson J, Vaughan SC: Sexual orientation and psychotherapy, in Oxford Textbook of Psychotherapy. Edited by Gabbard GO, Beck JS, Holmes J. Oxford, UK, Oxford University Press, 2005, pp 421–430

Pierce C: Stress analogs of racism and sexism: terrorism, torture, and disaster, in Mental Health, Racism, and Sexism. Edited by Willie C, Rieker P, Kramer B, et al. Pittsburgh, PA, University of Pittsburgh Press, 1995, pp 277–293

Price J, Price D, Williams G, et al: Changes in medical student attitudes as they progress through a medical course. J Med Ethics 24:110–117, 1998

PRMS: Risk management tips for physician bloggers. Psychiatric News 44:31, 2009

Rabjohn PA, Yager J: The effective resident work-hour regulation and psychiatry. Am J Psychiatry 165:308–311, 2008

Recupero PR: E-mail and the psychiatrist-patient relationship. J Am Acad Psychiatry Law 33:465–475, 2005

Reed DA, West CP, Mueller PS, et al: Behaviors of highly professional resident physicians. JAMA 300:1326–1333, 2008

Relman AS: Medical professionalism in the commercialized healthcare market. JAMA 298:2668–2670, 2007

Riser SJ, Banner RS: The charter on medical professionalism and the limits of medical power. Ann Intern Med 138:844–846, 2002

Roberts LW: Ethical dimensions of psychiatric research: a constructive, criterion-based approach to protocol preparation. The Research Protocol Ethics Assessment Tool (RePEAT). Biol Psychiatry 46:1106–1119, 1999

Roberts LW: Ethics as endeavor in psychiatry: principles, skills, and evidence. Psychiatric Times 19:33–36, 2002a

Roberts LW: Informed consent and the capacity for voluntarism. Am J Psychiatry 159:705–712, 2002b

Roberts LW: Ethical principles and skills in the care of mental illness. FOCUS 1:339–344, 2003

Roberts LW, Dyer AR: Concise Guide to Ethics in Mental Health Care. Washington, DC, American Psychiatric Publishing, 2004

Roberts LW, Hardee JT, Franchini G, et al: Medical students as patients: a pilot study of their health care needs, practices, and concerns. Acad Med 71:1225–1232, 1996

Roberts LW, McCarty T, Obenshain SS: Comprehensive performance examination gives insights into the "hidden curriculum." Acad Med 74:597–598, 1999

Roberts LW, Warner TD, Lyketsos C, et al: Perceptions of academic vulnerability associated with personal illness: a study of 1,027 students at nine medical schools. Collaborative Research Group on Medical Student Health. Compr Psychiatry 42:1–15, 2001

Roberts LW, Green Hammond KA, Geppert CM, et al: The positive role of professionalism and ethics training in medical education: a comparison of medical student and resident perspectives. Acad Psychiatry 28:17–182, 2004

Roberts LW, Geppert CM, Warner TD, et al: Becoming a good doctor: perceived need for ethics training focused on practical and professional development topics. Acad Psychiatry 29:301–309, 2005a

Roberts LW, Geppert CM, Warner TD, et al: Bioethics principles, informed consent, and ethical care for special populations: curricular needs expressed by men and women physicians-in-training. Psychosomatics 46:440–450, 2005b

Roberts LW, Johnson M, Brems C, et al: Preferences of Alaska and New Mexico psychiatrists regarding professionalism and ethics training. Acad Psychiatry 30:200–204, 2006

Rosen J: The Web means the end of forgetting. The New York Times Magazine, July 21, 2010, pp 30–37, 44–45

Rosenstein AH, O'Daniel M: Disruptive behavior and clinical outcomes: perceptions of nurses and physicians. Am J Nurs 105:54–64, 2005

Rosenstein AH, O'Daniel M: A survey of the impact of disruptive behaviors and communication defects on patient safety. Jt Comm J Qual Patient Saf 34:464–470, 2008

Røvik JO, Tyssen R, Hem E, et al: Job stress in young physicians with an emphasis on the work-home interface: a nine-year, nationwide and longitudinal study of its course and predictors. Ind Health 45:662–671, 2007

Schindler BA, Novack DH, Cohen DG, et al: The impact of the changing health care environment on the health and well-being of faculty at four medical schools. Acad Med 81:27–34, 2006

Schwartz A, Kotwicki RJ, McDonald WM: Developing a modern standard to define and assess professionalism in trainees. Acad Psychiatry 33:442–450, 2009

Seeman MV, Seeman M, Seeman B, et al: E-psychiatry: using Web-based communications to connect with patients. Psychiatric Times 27:1–7, February 8, 2010

Shapiro Y, Gabbard GO: A reconsideration of altruism from an evolutionary and psychodynamic perspective. Ethics Behav 4:23–42, 1994

Shapiro J, Miller R: How medical students think about ethical issues. Acad Med 69:591–593, 1994

Simon RI: Clinical Psychiatry and the Law. Washington DC, American Psychiatric Press, 1992

Simon RJ, Fleiss JL, Gurland BJ, et al: Depression and schizophrenia in black and white mental patients. Arch Gen Psychiatry 28:509–512, 1973

Sox HC: Medical professionalism and the parable of the craft guilds. Ann Intern Med 147:809–810, 2007

Spickard A, Gabbe SG, Christensen JF: Midcareer burnout in generalist and specialist physicians. JAMA 288:1447–1450, 2002

Stern DT (ed): Measuring Medical Professionalism. Oxford, UK, Oxford University Press, 2006

Stone B: Is Facebook growing up too fast? New York Times, March 29, 2009, Sunday Business, p 1

Strasburger LH, Jorgenson L, Sutherland P: The prevention of psychotherapist sexual misconduct: avoiding the slippery slope. Am J Psychother 46:544–555, 1992

Tarkan L: Arrogant, abusive, and disruptive—and a doctor. The New York Times, December 2, 2008, p D1

Thompson LA, Dawson K, Ferdig R, et al: The intersection of online social networking with medical professionalism. J Gen Intern Med 23:954–957, 2008

Tseng W-S, Streltzer J: Cultural Competence in Clinical Psychiatry. Washington, DC, American Psychiatric Publishing, 2004

Tyssen R, Dolatowski FC, Røvik JO, et al: Personality traits and types predict medical school stress: a 6-year longitudinal and nationwide study. Med Educ 41:781–787, 2007

Vaillant GE: Ego Mechanisms of Defense: A Guide for Clinicians and Researchers. Washington, DC, American Psychiatric Press, 1992

Vamos M: The concept of appropriate professional boundaries in psychiatric practice: a pilot training course. Aust N Z J Psychiatry 35:613–618, 2001 van Mook WNKA, Gorter SL, deGrave WS, et al: Bad apples spoil the barrel: addressing unprofessional behavior. Med Teach 32:891–898, 2010

Wagner P, Hendrich J, Moseley G, et al: Defining medical professionalism: a qualitative study. Med Educ 41:288–294, 2007

Warner TD, Gluck JP: What do we really know about conflicts of interest in biomedical research? Psychopharmacol (Berl) 171:36–46, 2003

Warner TD, Roberts LW: Scientific integrity, fidelity and conflicts of interest in research. Curr Opin Psychiatry 17:381–385, 2004

Wazana A: Physicians and the pharmaceutical industry: is a gift ever just a gift? JAMA 283:373–378, 2000

Wear D, Aultman JN (eds): Professionalism in Medicine: Critical Perspectives. New York, Springer, 2006

Weber DO: Poll results: doctors' disruptive behavior disturbs physician leaders. Physician Executive, Sept-Oct 2004, pp 6–14

Welner A, Liss JL, Robins E: Psychiatric symptoms in white and black inpatients, II: follow-up study. Compr Psychiatry 14:483–488, 1973

White H: Locating clinical boundaries in the World Wide Web. Am J Psychiatry 166:620–621, 2009

Wofford MM, Wofford JL, Bothra J, et al: Patients' complaints about physicians' behaviors: a qualitative study. Acad Med 79:134–138, 2004

Word CO, Zanna MP, Cooper J: The nonverbal mediation of self-fulfilling prophecies in interracial interaction. J Exp Soc Psychol 10:109–120, 1974

World Health Organization Department of Mental Health and Substance Abuse: Disease Control Priorities Related to Mental, Neurological, Developmental and Substance Abuse Disorders. Geneva, Switzerland, World Health Organization, 2006. Available at: http://whqlibdoc.who.int/publications/2006/924156332X_eng.pdf. Accessed February 18, 2008.

Index

*Page numbers printed in **boldface** type refer to tables or figures.*